The DEATHLESS STORY OF THE TITANIC

COMPLETE NARRATIVE WITH MANY ILLUSTRATIONS

FILMORE

ISBN 1-85044-067-0

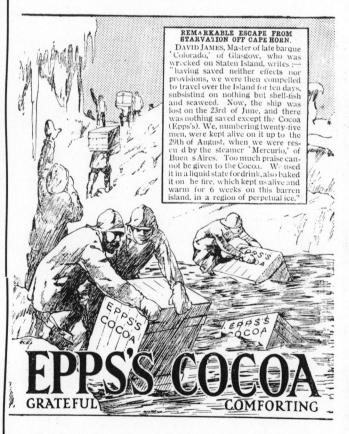

The DEATHLESS STORY
OF THE
TITANIC

A FACSIMILE REPRINT

LONDON · NEW YORK · HAMBURG · HONG KONG

Lloyd's of London Press Ltd

Preface

Great Bentley in Essex is not particularly associated with maritime history although it lies just a few miles away from the head office of Lloyd's of London Press Ltd. which moved to Colchester in 1974.

Mr Roy Warboys was therefore quite surprised to come across a yellowing periodical which proclaimed itself as *The Deathless Story of the Titanic* in the attic of his home. Not unnaturally he assumed an association between the publishers, Lloyd's Weekly News, and Lloyd's of London and being a man greatly interested in history and antiques, decided to pursue some enquiries through the husband of his wife's friend, Mr Clifford Mullinger, Computer Operations Manager at Lloyd's of London Press.

The 72-year-old supplement aroused intense interest among the staff at LLP but defeated the knowledge of several members who had long studied both company and Corporation of Lloyd's history. Finally, thanks to the help of Lloyd's of London chief librarian, Mr Terry Dinan, it was identified as the product of a rival maritime publishing company, long since departed from the commercial scene.

If relationships between the rivals were less than amicable at the time – for such is rumoured to be the case – the time had come to give credit where credit was due.

This facsimile, as near to the original as the printers are able to achieve with modern technology and paper sizes, is published with full acknowledgements to those contemporary writers, editors, publishers and printers.

Our thanks go, too, to the few companies remaining who have consented to the reproduction of their advertisements. Bovril UK points out that it no longer claims miracles of physiology for its product which remains a fine, healthy drink!

July 1985   Lloyd's of London Press Ltd.

Introduction

On the moonless night of 15 April 1912, for reasons which are still heatedly debated, the S.S. *Titanic* struck an iceberg and slid slowly beneath the black Atlantic Ocean.

More than 1,600 passengers and crew perished with her, men, women and children. The richest of the rich and the poorest of the poor. When the news reached London and New York there were scenes which, today, television would have brought to our living rooms, of anguished families clamouring for news, half-hysterical, half in disbelief that the majestic and reputedly unsinkable pride of the White Star Line, could have met with such disaster.

With no television and limited radio it took weeks for the full scale of the tragedy to become known. Once it was known it remained indelibly printed upon the minds of the two nations which suffered the greatest loss, Britain and the United States of America, and a subject of intense curiosity for much of the rest of the world. In the United States today there exists still a huge organisation, The Titanic Historical Society, devoted to pursuing every scrap of information available on the disaster. The hope, and indeed the faith, that something as yet unknown will be turned up to resolve the final responsibility for the loss of the *Titanic*, never fades.

The lengthy and painstaking British inquiry into the loss has been scathingly put down as a "whitewash" by writers who have devoted many years of their lives to research into the disaster. Equally, its findings have been vigorously upheld by others, including survivors of the tragedy.

The passing of time changes the complexion of all the arguments. *The Deathless Story of the Titanic* is a contemporary view of events. Its contributors were professional journalists concerned, within the limitations of available communications, to present the fact of the matter though, of course, in a manner which would elicit the closest attention of the reader.

In publishing this facsimile there is no intention to make a stance on the side of these writers, nor those who would refute their reports. This is how it seemed at the time.

There have been greater tragedies since, incurring far greater loss of life, which have not lived on so vividly in the minds of men. In the cynical latter half of the century it is perhaps easy to see why. The story of the *Titanic* is, as so aptly predicted, deathless, because it encompassed everything the human being finds fascinating. Death, grief, wealth, beauty, heroism and intrigue. The loss of the *Titanic* demonstrated more surely than any other single event in history two unchallengeable facts. Death is the great equaliser and Man, for all his pride and genius, remains the plaything of the Elements.

Patricia Morris

The Deathless Story of the "Titanic."

By PHILIP GIBBS.

I.

Pomp and splendour, pride and pow'r
Vanished in a little hour;
Not a bubble left to show
All the skill that rusts below;
Launched the wonder of the world,
To unfathomed ruin hurl'd.

II.

Yet a glory hovers there
In the bright Atlantic air,
Yet a blessing burns the wave
O'er leviathan's huge grave:
Women saw that glory flow,
Children saw that blessing glow.

III.

When our utmost has been done
Under moon and under sun,
When our strength has piled its might
To the dazzlement of sight,
Waits the matchless deed of all,
For another's sake to fall.

IV.

Happy wheresoe'er they be,
Those whose bodies strew the sea,
Those who to themselves were dead
While they toiled in others' stead,
Those who waved adieu, and then
Died like Christians and like men.

V.

Life were mean without great death,
Deeds that catch and hold the breath,
Acts that like a trumpet tear
Torpor from the stagnant air,
Hours that set the Inchcape bell,
Swinging over heav'n and hell.

HAROLD BEGBIE.

THE story of the sea is one long narrative of adventures, of heroes, of tragedies. Always, like some dreadful monster of old legend, the sea claims human sacrifice. Her bed is strewn with the broken fabric of great ships. Into her wide embrace of death she has dragged down brave men and fair women and little children since first the human race ventured out upon her waters.

But never in the long tale of tragedy has the relentless ocean claimed so great a ship as the "Titanic," nor seized so terrible a toll of human life in one great sum of death, as the number of those who, in the moment of supreme agony, were hurled into the ice-cold waters of the Atlantic. The sinking of the "Titanic," greatest of the world's great ships, stands alone in its awfulness, supreme in tragedy.

Humanity has not yet recovered from the shock to its heart and conscience which stirred it with horror when the dreadful news was first whispered across the world, when unbelief that such a thing could be was followed by dreadful certainty, when the last rays of hope were extinguished by black despair, and when at last, after a long delay, as it seemed to those who counted time by heart-throbs, the plain, appalling facts were made known to the world.

The tears of those who have to weep for their dead are not yet dry. Not yet has our imagination blotted out the frightful vision of that mighty ship rising up "like a black finger pointing through the darkness" before plunging into the abyss. We are still haunted by that death-ship and hear the great chorus of human agony which rose into the silence of that night of doom. It seems as though we may never thrust from our eyes that ghastly vision nor deafen our ears to those despairing cries.

Yet greater than the tragedy is the glory. Whatever may have been the human pride and error that sent the "Titanic" upon her first voyage, and her last, upon a dangerous course, at a perilous speed, and with a false security in her power over the forces of Nature—these things await judgment—human character has revealed itself with its old qualities of nobility, which for a time seemed sleeping, has made a great affirmation of faith, has gained and held victory over death itself.

In a few hours of the night there were done upon that ice-strewn sea deeds which will not pass into the great forgetfulness, but will shine with a bright light above all the failures and futilities of life, and ring down the ages like an heroic song. Before the doomed ship was engulfed in the devouring waters there was a drama upon her decks more wonderful in its dignity and splendour than any that has been invented by imagination. All the great virtues of the soul were here displayed upon "that dim dark sea, so like unto death"—courage, self-forgetfulness, self-sacrifice, love, devotion to those highest ideals which are the guiding stars of life, beyond the common reach. Heroism, not tawdry, touched by no falsity of melodrama, but simple, with a divine simplicity, leapt forth, as though to the call of God, like a "sunburst in the storm of death."

These people had not much time for heroism. They had to think swiftly, to decide swiftly, to act swiftly. Without wasting time in dreadful doubt, in frightful hesitations, in the perplexity of despair, they made the most of the time allowed them by the hurrying pursuit of death, and they filled it to the brim, and crowded it with valour, with sweet and noble acts. Men and women vied with each other in the courtesies of courage, in helpfulness, in renunciation, in loyalty, and in love. The "Titanic" became the shrine of many miracles, for there is no greater miracle than this, that a man should lay down his life for his friend; that weak women should suddenly be uplifted from their weakness and become strong to suffer and to dare; that men unused to hardihood, untrained to peril, born and bred in luxury, as many of them were, should rise above all temptations of fear and baseness, and obey to the last letter the great code of honour.

Temptations of fear there must have been. It is idle to think that all these people were by nature heroic, made of the stuff of heroes and heroines. It was not easy for them to die. They, like all of us, cherished the sweetness of life. Many of them, like many of us all, were by nature not heroical, but cowardly, in the face of death. They had drunk deep, these rich men and women, of the wine of life. They had known all that is most beautiful, most excellent in life. Numbers of them had been the darlings of fortune. All of them, humble and exalted in rank, had looked forward to years of happiness with those they loved.

No, it was not easy for any of them to die, and when the call came, spoken by the voice of Death across the waters, the hearts of some of them must have been wracked with an agony beyond words or tears, and their eyes must have been blind with fear.

The brave man is not he who feels no fear,
For that were stupid and irrational,
But he whose noble soul its fear subdues
And bravely dares the danger nature shrinks from.

That was the sublime courage on the "Titanic." These delicate women, these young brides, and American heiresses, and English emigrants, women made of the same clay as their sisters in all the streets of life, and therefore no more courageous by training or quality, not picked in any way for the supreme test of courage, subdued their fears, and were quiet and calm in those awful hours. As they went into the boats from the side of that vast ship, which had seemed an impregnable fortress against all the forces of the wind and weather, and parted from their husbands after a last good-bye spoken in the darkness, there went up no shrieks of despair, no wild hysterical wailing, no madness of grief. By a great mercy many of them believed that they would again see their men. They did not know that they had left them without a chance. But they knew well enough, too well, indeed, that they were all in the deadliest of peril.

"Women and children first"—the old law of the sea was obeyed. The old tradition of chivalry was upheld, as splendidly as ever in the story of the sea. It was disobeyed only by women who refused, by a right not to be denied them if they claim it, to be separated from those without whom life would be worse than death.

But what now of the men who had stayed behind? They surely may take their place upon the roll-call of immortal honour. The few who survived have told the story of their comrades, though not all the story. In that immense ship, a floating tide of human life, there were many hiding places of heroism, many streets in which men's bravery was unobserved by any one who lived to tell the tale.

But a few names have been made glorious among the many who were no less worthy. The wireless operator who died at his post, working still when the water was up to his waist, doing his duty until Death touched him on the shoulder; millionaires like Colonel Astor, brave gentlemen like Major Butt, simple, honest seamen like Captain Smith—most luckless of all sea-captains; such a brilliant journalist and greathearted man as W. T. Stead; and the bandmaster Hartley, with his fellow musicians, who played the requiem of the "Titanic" and their hymn of faith, to the very threshold of eternity, are secure of deathless renown, and will never be forgotten so long as the story of the "Titanic" has power to thrill the hearts of men.

They helped the women into the boats with cheery words, with quiet discipline, with the spirit which lives in the fine flower of chivalry. They checked the least sign of panic, and then as they waved a last farewell to the women when the boats moved away like shadows across the water, they turned, and knew themselves to be within a little while of death.

The Hope of Rescue.

No doubt many of them hoped that rescue would reach them in time. They knew that soundless words were speeding for hundreds of miles on circling waves of invisibility, calling for help. Some of them could hear, perhaps, the throb of the electric spark flashing the wireless messages through the spacious darkness. Hope, even though a faint, flickering hope, must have been alight in many hearts. And faith, too, helped them to put a grip upon their nerves and thrust down the demons of fear. They could hardly believe that this mighty ship, in whose great fortress they had roamed, of whose strength they had been proud, which had been called a thousand times "unsinkable," was so mortally wounded by the stabbing ice that it would plunge to death beneath them. So some of them may have clung to these straws of hope. But they also knew that death was very close to them. They could see its shadow creeping upon them, deeper than the darkness of the night. They had time to think and time to be afraid.

But we know that they stifled fear and made the great conquest of their human weakness. Down below the engineers stood by their posts. They knew the worst, if others did not know. But not one of them abandoned his post of duty, not one of them came up to seek a chance of life. Patiently, with sublime courage, they waited for death. The postmen of the "Titanic" spent their last hour in trying to rescue their mail bags. They, too, remembered Nelson's watchword, and did their duty to the end, faithful unto death.

On the decks stood a few women clasping their husbands in the last embrace. Gentlemen of England and America stood shoulder to shoulder, like fellow soldiers in the face of the enemy. Sixteen hundred human souls, or more, listened to the summons of Death knocking at their hearts, and sixteen hundred human souls, or more, behaved themselves decorously and with a wonderful dignity in those moments of silent agony. The "Titanic" kept her lights burning. Tier upon tier, those little stars gleamed in the darkness, each one of them a golden sign of the courage that kept the engineers "down below." The captain was upon his bridge, the officers at their stations. And when the last moment came and the finger of doom touched the "Titanic," Death heard music upon this ship. Loud and

clear across the dark waters sounded the hymn of faith, "Nearer, my God, to Thee." That music, divine as an angelic melody when played by men face to face with eternity, was silenced only when the ship reared up in her death agony, and then plunged into the depths. A great cry of human bitterness went up to the eternal silence. The black sea was alive with struggling figures. . . . In a little while there was quietude and peace. Where the "Titanic" had floated like a grand palace with many lighted windows there was no ruffle of the waves, no shadow of her greatness. The mightiest, proudest of the world's ships had disappeared for ever and "left not a wrack behind." Sixteen hundred souls had gone to meet their God. Oh, pitiful tragedy! Oh, splendour of human courage! Oh, mystery of human life!

In all its facts of horror and of heroism the story of the "Titanic" will put a spell upon the imagination of men, for it has a spiritual significance, and will stand as a great tradition. It must be told, so that our children and our children's children will cherish its memory as a sacred trust, as a tremendous warning, and as an heroic inspiration. Here in these pages it is told as fully as it has been recorded by many witnesses, and as the facts have been gathered from all trustworthy accounts. It is a narrative which one day must be told by a master hand, so that it may remain as one of the epic stories of the sea.

THE "TITANIC" SETS OUT FROM SOUTHAMPTON.

The ship was cheered, the harbour cleared.
Merrily did we drop
Below the kirk, below the hill,
Below the lighthouse top.

The sun came up upon the left,
Out of the sea came he !
And he shone bright, and on the right
Went down into the sea.

On Wednesday, April 10, 1912, the White Star liner "Titanic" started on her maiden voyage from Southampton to New York.

A crowd had gathered on the pier to watch that great ship leave her moorings, and as she began to move in her immensity cheers rolled out across the waters in a great chorus of pride and triumph. The band was playing a merry tune on deck, and passengers, leaning over the rails, waved farewell greetings to their friends and gave answering cheers. On her way out from Southampton the "Titanic" had a triumphant progress, towering tremendously above all the craft, which seemed so dwarf-like as the shadow of her great hull passed across them on the glittering waters.

The setting out upon this maiden voyage seemed to mark a new era in the story of ships and the sea. There were men and women at Southampton whose hearts were uplifted by a sense of gladness and pride. For they knew, as experts and as lovers of ships, the power, the splendour, and the majesty of the "Titanic." Some of them had watched the building of the vessel since first her keel plate was laid on March 31, 1909, in Harland and Wolff's shipbuilding yard at Belfast. Many of them had explored her vastness and seen all the treasures of her luxury when a year afterwards she was fully framed and launched on May 31, 1911. Only a few days before this beginning of her first voyage a large number of visitors had roamed into all parts of this greatest liner in the world, and had described it as the most astounding achievement in naval architecture and marine engineering.

For never was there such a ship as this. From keel to navigating bridge she rose to a sheer height of 104 feet. "The heaviest sea," said one of the officers, "can never wash aboard. . . . We may laugh at dirty weather." She was 1,000 feet long, so that as she swung round she looked like a moving fortress. She had a registered tonnage of 46,328 tons, which was over 1,000 tons more than the next largest ship in the world, her sister, the "Olympic."

Everything in her construction was upon a tremendous scale. The strength of the shell was like that of a castle with massive walls of steel. Her plates were six feet wide and thirty feet long. In the building up of every part of her, stability and strength were the one consideration. Right throughout the hull were steel girders, beams, and stanchions, like pillars of a cathedral, to give her absolute rigidity in the heaviest sea. A double bottom, riveted by hydraulic power, seemed to ensure absolute safety, even though she ripped herself by striking something under water.

A system of water-tight bulkhead doors had been designed by Lord Pirrie and his marine architects, with a massive construction which seemed to defy the greatest danger. "Each

door," said the owners' description, "is held in the open position by a suitable friction clutch, which can be instantly released by means of a powerful electric magnet controlled from the captain's bridge, so that, in the event of accident, or at any time when it might be considered advisable, the captain can, by simply moving an electric switch, instantly close the doors throughout—*practically making the vessel unsinkable.*"

Those words in italics, written in the official description, read now with a dreadful irony.

But, as though to make assurance doubly sure, there were additional means of closing the bulkhead doors. They could not only be shut immediately from below by one lever, but as a further precaution floats were provided beneath the floor level, which, in the event of water accidentally entering any of the compartments, would automatically close the doors opening into that compartment, if they had not already been dropped by the captain or his officers.

A ladder of escape was provided in each boiler-room, engine-room, and similar water-tight compartments, so that the closing of the doors should not imprison any men, though the risk of that was lessened by electric bells placed near each door, which would ring the alarm before they shut against the invading waters.

Some Details of the "Titanic."—1 and 2. The Sitting Room and Bedroom in one of the "Millionaire Suites." 3. The Promenade Deck, showing the lifeboats, from a photograph taken at Queenstown when the ship left land for the last time. 4. A photograph comparing the huge side of the ship with the tender at Queenstown. 5. The Verandah Café. 6. The Parisian Café.

"The 'Titanic' could not sink." "The 'Titanic' is unsinkable." These words were repeated again and again by men of expert knowledge, who rejoiced in their belief that science had conquered over Nature and that the sea would be cheated of any further sacrifice.

Within the great vessel was a tremendous power of activity, so that her vast weight might be driven forward, at the speed of a railway train, through the most tumultuous sea. She carried twenty-nine huge boilers, with 159 furnaces placed in watertight compartments, which could be isolated by the devices already explained. For her electric lighting she carried four engines and dynamos generating a vast voltage of electricity, so that from stem to stern this mighty vessel might blaze with brilliant lamps.

So in power, almost terrifying to the imagination, the "Titanic" was incomparable. But in beauty and luxury also she had no rival. All that the genius of modern life has invented for comfort and adornment was lavished upon her in a prodigal spirit; all that wealth and art can attain in splendour was given to her decoration. The imagination of old story-tellers writing of fabulous ships paled before the actuality of this magnificence.

It seemed as if the builders of the "Titanic" had been riotous in their endeavour to make this greatest of ships the ultimate example of modern luxury beyond which it would be impossible to go. On the ten decks you might forget the cares of life, the squalor and ugliness of life, even the duties of life, and in this sea-palace of the Titanic queen spend the days of the voyage in continual pleasure and delight. These sound like words of exaggeration, but the "Titanic" was herself an exaggeration of ordinary things.

Luxury on the Liner.

Here any passenger might sit in a tropical verandah restaurant, where vines grew upon the lattice work of windows through which there streamed—artificial sunlight! It was called the Café Parisien, and here at night the band played the gayest tunes of life—French chansons, and American ragtime dances, and the light melodies which charm away the shadows of the soul—until suddenly the tune changed one night into that hymn which has become more sacred since.

Here was a gymnasium, splendidly equipped, so that men might counteract the effects of luxury by strenuous exercise. There was a racquet court for ladies and gentlemen of active mood. Turkish and electric baths and a great swimming bath, luxuriously appointed, were provided for first and second class passengers.

The dining-rooms, staterooms, and common rooms were furnished in various periods and styles, copied faithfully from old models, so that English gentlemen might sit in rooms panelled and adorned like those of Haddon Hall, and fair women might have their beauty reflected in oval mirrors hanging upon walls like those of Versailles when Marie Antoinette played with her ladies. For the payment of £870 per voyage the richest man on earth would not lack a single comfort that his wealth might buy.

Even the third class dining saloon, seating 500 passengers, and the other third class accommodation was as richly and beautifully decorated as though kings and queens were on the third class list.

There had been economy only in one thing by those who built the ship and furnished her. They had economised in boats and rafts. It seemed so foolish to carry boats when the "Titanic" was "unsinkable." Alas! the pity of it! Humanity has paid dearly for that economy.

THE HUMAN FREIGHT OF THE GREAT SHIP.

As slow our ship her foamy track
Against the wind was cleaving,
Her trembling pennant still look'd back
To that dear isle 'twas leaving.
So loth we part from all we love,
From all the links that bind us;
So turn our hearts, as on we rove,
To those we've left behind us.

So the "Titanic" steamed out of Southampton to touch at Queenstown, and then go Westward-Ho! for New York. The world's Press wrote panegyrics on her power and glory. There were many who envied the lucky ones who had obtained a passage on this ship of pleasure for her maiden voyage. We were lifted up by a new pride in the genius of shipbuilding.

Upon leaving Queenstown the number of persons on board was 2,358, made up as follow :—

First class passengers	350
Second class passengers	305
Steerage passengers	800
Crew	903

The "Titanic" was commanded by Captain E. J. Smith, commodore of the White Star Fleet, and one of the most popular officers among all ocean-going lines.

Sixty-two years of age, he was the very type of a British sea-captain, quiet, with shrewd, keen eyes beneath his shaggy brows, strong in command, gentle in social converse, modest as a simple seaman, brave as a lion, of unblemished honour. He was a Staffordshire man, who had an early apprenticeship at sea in the ships of Gibson and Company, and took his master's certificate at twenty-five years of age. He had sailed in many seas, suffered in many storms, tasted all the salt of a seaman's life before he began his career with the White Star Line in 1886. He became chief officer of the "Cufic," and two years later was promoted as captain of the "Celtic."

As vessels increased in size and power, Captain Smith changed from one ship to another, and bore the burden of increasing responsibility. He commanded seventeen White Star liners in succession, and he was known and loved all over the world by men and women who had travelled with him. His employers had absolute faith in his skill and judgment, in his caution and strength of character, in his unswerving fidelity to duty.

Then came his first stroke of ill-luck, when the "Olympic," under his command collided with H.M.S. "Hawke" in the Solent. At the enquiry which followed Captain Smith was exonerated from all blame, the White Star Line were not shaken in their faith in his ability, and he was chosen without hesitation for the honour of commanding their newest and greatest vessel. So did he stand upon the bridge of the "Titanic," and as yet the world heard nothing of those doubts which came to the mind of superstitious men—and seamen of all men are superstitious—who shook their heads and said, "Captain Smith has broken his luck."

Never had any captain been responsible for the safety of passengers representing such immense wealth as those who went with the "Titanic."

Some Famous Passengers.

Among the first-class passengers was a group of rich Americans whose fortunes amounted to at least £120,000,000. Great merchants, the princes of trade, the controllers of the world's markets, they assembled at dinner on the first night of the voyage with a great gathering of men and women to whom life had given its best gifts. Not only wealth was represented here, but intellectual ability and great qualities of character.

Among the most famous Americans were Colonel John Jacob Astor, a member of one of the wealthiest families in the world, and a gallant man who served with honour in the Spanish-American war, when he presented a mountain battery to the Government for use in the campaign; Major Archibald Butt, aide-de-camp to President Taft, and the one man in America who lent a little touch of pageantry in his uniform to the democratic simplicity at the White House; Mr. Washington Dodge, a member of a great American banking firm; Mr. Benjamin Guggenheim, a member of a family of capitalists associated with Mr. Pierpont Morgan; Mr. Harry Harris, theatrical manager; Mr. Washington Roebling, head of a great wire cable firm; Mr. J. B. Thayer, president of the Pennsylvania Railway; Mr. Isidor Straus, a wealthy merchant and great philanthropist; Mr. George D. Widener, son of the Philadelphia millionaire who recently bought "The Mill," by Rembrandt, from Lord Lansdowne; Mr. Clarence Moore, a famous archæologist and traveller; Mr. Frank D. Millet, a celebrated American artist; Mr. Charles Melville Hays, president of the Grand Trunk Railway; and Mr. C. Clarence Jones, a big stockbroker, of New York.

Among the English passengers there was no more brilliant personality than Mr. W. T. Stead, undoubtedly the greatest journalist of the age. A man of keenest and most penetrating intellect when dealing with many subjects of life, a man of large enthusiasms, of high ideals, of restless energy, and with a great gift of laughter, he was a shining light in any kind of company, and made innumerable friends in all ranks of society and in all countries. In spite of strange spiritual beliefs in which he showed the greatest credulity, he was honoured as a man of noble integrity, and an unswerving faith in all that is best in human nature.

Among his other fellow passengers were Mr. Bruce Ismay, chairman of the White Star Line; Mr. Thomas Andrews, jun., managing director of Messrs. Harland and Wolff, the builders of the "Titanic"; Mr. Christopher Head, ex-mayor of Chelsea; the Countess of Rothes, who was going to America to meet her husband, a representative peer of Scotland; Lady Duff Gordon, famous as a society "modiste" under the name of Lucile, and her husband, Sir Cosmo Duff Gordon. There were many other people of interesting personality, of good fortune, and of good hope.

The Captain of the "Titanic" and some of his Officers:—1. W. M. Murdock, first mate, who was in charge on the bridge when the ship struck. 2. Captain Smith with his pet dog. 3. H. W. McElroy, chief purser. 4. H. F. Wilde, chief mate 5. Dr. J. E. Simpson, the ship's surgeon. 6. H. J. Lowe, fifth mate. 7. F. Evans, one of the look-out men. 8. H. J Pitman, third mate.

Some of them were making this voyage a honeymoon trip, and there were many young husbands and wives happy in their loves. Colonel and Mrs. Astor were returning from their honeymoon tour in Egypt, Mr. and Mrs. Marvin from their wedding tour in England, Mr. and Mrs. Beane had married in Norwich three days before joining the "Titanic," Mr. and Mrs. Marshall were on their way to a honeymoon in California, Mr. and Mrs. M'Namee, one of the branch managers of Lipton's, had been married a month, and with his wife was going to a post in New York.

There was all the drama of life within that floating city, all that interchange of social courtesies, all those beginnings of pleasant friendships, all those partnerships of love which are to be found on a transatlantic liner. Some of these men were busy, no doubt, with thoughts and schemes of ambition, planning out their future as they paced the decks, smoking quietly in the darkness and peace of night. Busy life lay in front of them. They saw no sudden end to all their dreams and visions and hopes. If they were old and tired they renewed their youthfulness by watching the love couples, the young mothers with their children, the gaiety of many young men and women who played the games provided so abundantly to cure boredom and relieve the monotony of life on board ship.

In gallant trim the stately vessel goes,
Youth on the prow and Pleasure at the helm.

In the evening, when the shadows crept over the waters, and twilight deepened into the darkness, and the star-strewn sky glimmered above, this great vessel, stealing so quietly and swiftly on her way, seemed like a dream-ship. To lovers who clasped hands on some lonely part of one of the decks there came the sound of singing from the saloon, borne faintly across the waters, with the throbbing notes of stringed instruments. This beauty and this life on the sea steal into the senses, and the spirit of the ship seems to put a spell upon its passengers.

My soul is an enchanted ship,
Which like a sleeping swan doth float
Upon the silver waves of thy sweet singing,
And thine doth like an angel sit
Beside the helm conducting it,
Whilst all the winds with melody are ringing.

So may heart have spoken to heart upon the "Titanic" before the voice of doom was heard out of the silence of the sea.

Some of the friendships formed by men whom the strings of fate had drawn together on the "Titanic" lasted until death, though not very long. One of them has been recorded. It was between W. T. Stead and Frederick K. Seward, a famous New York lawyer. Mr. Seward has related some of the last conversations of a man who delighted in conversation, and that table-talk as the ship sped on her way to destruction has a haunting interest.

Unfinished Conversations.

Mr. Seward sat at Purser McIlroy's table, and next to him was the English journalist. The party at table consisted of eight persons, six of them Englishmen. Of those half-dozen Mr. Seward is the sole survivor. Those who were privileged to know Mr. Stead may seem to hear his voice as he told his new friend of a disturbing dream which had come to him in the night. It was an incoherent, nonsensical dream about somebody persistently throwing cats out of a top-storey window, but it had curiously impressed him. It even induced him to lend Mr. Seward a book by Dr. Blackmore, which, he laughingly said, was calculated to make any reader dream to distraction.

On another occasion Mr Stead talked in delightful fashion about the great American newspaper proprietor—"Willie Hearst, my own product," as he called him. "Years ago," he said, "in Hearst's earlier days, when he was developing his sensational newspaper, I was with him in his office an hour. I asked him if he had a soul, for that was what American journalism needed most. Hearst looked surprised, but from that day onward there was scarcely a single journalistic decision which he did not discuss with me."

Mr. Stead also spoke a great deal of the public difficulties he had to face for nearly a generation, especially the opprobrium heaped upon him owing to his opposition to the South African War. He gave what to Mr. Seward and to most people who were not in England in those days would have seemed an incredible description of the sinister persecution to which he and Mr. Lloyd George were subjected. He rejoiced that they had lived it down.

"I am afraid nobody living knows how he died," says Mr. Seward. "He was one of the very few who were actually on the deck when the iceberg was struck. I saw him soon afterwards, and was thoroughly scared, but he preserved a most beautiful composure. Whether he stayed on board or sought safety by leaping into the sea I cannot tell, but I do know he faced death with philosophic resignation. I deem it a privilege I shall prize for the rest of my days that I had the opportunity in the last hours of his life to hold converse with a great Englishman."

There were many unfinished conversations in the "Titanic," and they may only be continued in eternity. But at that time in the dining-rooms no one saw a spectre at the feast. It was a ship of laughter and lightheartedness.

THE DANGER ZONE OF FLOATING ICE.

In the first watch of the night,
Without a signal's sound,
Out of the sea, mysteriously
The fleet of Death rose all around.

Yet as the "Titanic" steamed across the Atlantic every hour brought her closer to the danger zone unknown to all her passengers, not causing much anxiety, it seems, even to her captain and his officers. They were approaching the southernmost line of floating ice.

In America reports had already been received of a great ice-field with many bergs obstructing the west-bound Transatlantic highway.

The Cunard liner "Carmania," arriving in New York from Adriatic and Mediterranean ports, had run through the pack and had been in grave danger. The passengers had counted twenty-five icebergs, and one cluster was no further than 100 ft. away. The liner had had to feel her course for hours through an ice-lane.

Another vessel, the French liner "Niagara," did not escape unscathed. She was holed twice beneath the water-line and had some of her plates buckled. At one moment a wireless telegram was sent from her to the "Carmania" asking for help, but later the captain decided that he was able to navigate his ship to port, having patched up the damage to the hull. Similar reports were received from smaller vessels which had been damaged by ice. They had passed numerous "growlers"—large bergs that had melted on top until their upper surfaces were almost awash—which in bad or failing light were extremely difficult to discern.

What was happening was the early breaking up of the ice in the Arctic, which was passing down by the Labrador current. In the meteorological chart of the North Atlantic for April, issued by the Meteorological Office, the track recommended for steamers was towards a point about 300 miles south-east of Cape Race, just avoiding the ordinary limit for field ice surrounding Newfoundland. But by an unusual freak of nature that limit had extended further south in the month of April, and great bergs lay across the path of the southern route to New York.

On Friday, April 12, Captain Smith received a warning which was whispered across the waves to him. It was the first foreboding of peril. That message came from the captain of a French liner, the "Touraine," which on April 10, in latitude 45.15 North and longitude 50.40 West, entered an icefield at midnight. The "Touraine" emerged from the icefield at 1.15 a.m. The bergs were very low above the water. The same morning at 6 a.m. the French ship coasted along the southern edge of another icefield for three-quarters of an hour.

On Friday the "Touraine" was, she reports, in constant communication with the "Titanic" up to nine o'clock at night. M. Caussin, the commander, notified by wireless telegraphy the position of an iceberg he had encountered to the commander of the "Titanic." Captain Smith replied, also by wireless, "sincerely thanking him for his information."

Nearing the Ice.

But the sea was without a sign of peril around the "Titanic." There was no reason, it seemed, to be more vigilant than usual. "Although ice had been reported," said Mr. Lightoller, the second officer of the "Titanic," "I was not anxious about it." He did not consider it necessary to post an additional look-out.

Saturday passed and Sunday came, and there was merriment on board for those who had no duties in the ship. The hours slipped away, and when darkness descended over the waters there was still no sign of impending peril, except that the wind blew with an icy breath, so that many people were chilled in spite of the warmest wraps, and hurried down from the decks to the warmth and brilliance of the state rooms.

That drop in the temperature was caused by the presence of icebergs, still far away, but creeping with the current like the ghosts of white ships beyond the vision of those who kept watch on the great ship of life. No human eye had yet seen that one iceberg sunk deep, with sharp edges, below the level of the dark sea.

But Captain Smith had had another warning. It came from a steamer believed to be the "Amerika," reporting icebergs in that locality. The message gave the longitude, but not the latitude. The icebergs were reported between 49 deg. and 51 deg.

According to the evidence of Mr. Lightoller, the second officer, it was on Sunday afternoon at about one o'clock that the captain told him of these wireless messages. Mr. Lightoller was then on the bridge, having relieved First Officer Murdock, who had gone to lunch. When Mr. Murdock returned the second officer told him exactly what the captain had said, and he replied, "All right."

While the passengers were at dinner that evening Mr. Lightoller was back on the bridge, and at 8.55 o'clock he again saw Captain Smith, who joined him there. By this time both the officers were aware that they were approaching the danger zone.

"We spoke of the weather," said Mr. Lightoller in his evidence before the American Senate, "of the calmness of the sea, and the clearness of the night, and about the time we should be in getting to the vicinity of the ice. I was impressed,

and I had on my mind the proximity of the ice. The captain and I talked for about twenty-five minutes."

It was at 9.20 that the captain left the bridge, and he gave a final word to the officer of the watch.

"If you are in the slightest degree doubtful, let me know," he said.

"All right, sir," replied the Second Officer.

Before going off duty Mr. Lightoller sent word to the carpenter to look out for the fresh-water supply, as it might be in danger of freezing, and he gave the "crow's nest" a strict order to look out for icebergs.

When First Officer Murdock came upon the bridge to relieve his comrade they had a few words together. It was almost a repetition of the conversation with the captain.

"Murdock," said Mr. Lightoller, "remarked on the weather —how clear and calm it was, and the long distance we could see. It was so clear that you could see the stars setting down to the horizon."

In the Atlantic Danger Zone.—(1). The "Titanic" among the ice, a compound picture from a photograph of the liner, and a special drawing. (2.) Photograph and drawing to show a huge iceberg, of which nine-tenths are under water. (3.) The ice-field in which the "Titanic" was lost, photographed from the deck of another liner shortly before the disaster.

It was then very cold, being 31 deg. above zero, though not unsually cold for that longitude at that time of year. The "Titanic" was then heading for the vicinity of the southernmost ice. As far as it is known, speed had not been slackened, and the "Titanic" was travelling at over twenty knots an hour.

Meanwhile dinner had been finished below deck. There had been dancing among the first-class passengers; the band was still playing merry tunes. Three Frenchmen—M. Fernand Omont, a business man of Havre, M. Pierre Maréchal, an aviator, and M. Paul Chévre, a sculptor—were playing bridge with a Mr. Smith, of Philadelphia. There were other little card parties, and here and there small groups of men telling

their adventures and good stories before turning into bed.

It was ten o'clock at night, and many people, tired of pleasure, weary with the strong air of the sea, conscious of how long the days seem on board ship, in spite of all the entertainments, had already retired to their cabins and prepared for sleep.

The life of the "Titanic" was settling down for the quietude of the night, and all these tired people had as perfect a sense of security as though they were going to bed in a great hotel.

They had implicit faith in the safety of the ship, in the vigilance of the officers, in the caution of Captain Smith—that strong, calm, genial man, who now and again had strolled into the state-rooms with a cheery word or two.

But in that hour as they laid down to rest the finger of an Unseen Hand was pointing to the "Titanic" through the darkness of the night. An Unheard Voice was pronouncing the awful doom. The wings of the black bird of Death were already fluttering above that mighty vessel. To those who had gone to sleep that night fate was preparing a dreadful awakening, and many of those who had not yet closed their eyes would not sleep again until they had found eternal rest.

The "Titanic" in that hour was like a city preparing for peaceful slumber while the enemy is at her gates. Here in the cabins down the streets of this city at sea mothers were bending over sleeping babes, women were putting off their finery, youth was already in the land of dreams, old age was praying for a good night's sleep.

Within the high steel walls of the "Titanic" all that civilisation means, all that human life means, was here gathered up. The rich men of the world, the heirs and heiresses of great fortunes, lay a few decks away from Irish emigrants and from the people of poverty. All sorts and conditions of men, the whole scale of social life, the whole gamut of human emotions, were here enclosed in that palace-ship; and, though they knew it not, in a little while wealth and poverty, youth and old age would be made equal before the face of eternity.

have been under any illusion. Without knowing the full extent of the damage, he knew that his "luck" had gone, and that the proud ship under his command had received a terrible blow. But this sea-captain did not falter or show any sign of that despair which must have filled his heart more rapidly than the water filled his ship. Quiet, calm, decisive, he went about his duty from now until the end. He remains a sublime figure of simplicity and courage.

His next order from the bridge is reported by Robert Hichens, who still stood at the wheel:—

"Send to the carpenter and tell him to sound the ship."

The message was sent to the carpenter, but he never came up to report. He was probably the first man to lose his life.

By this time a large number of people in the ship had been startled from their sleep and from their amusements by the shock which had shaken the vessel and by the stopping of the engines. It was not a great shock. Mr. Lightoller, the second officer, who had been in his cabin but was not asleep, described it as "a slight grinding, and then a shock, with very little noise." He went up on deck, where he met the third officer, to whom he spoke, declaring that they must have struck an iceberg. Then he saw the captain on the bridge with Mr. Murdock by his side.

Other people came on deck. Among them were the three Frenchmen who had been playing auction bridge with Mr. Smith, of Philadelphia.

"We were talking cheerfully when suddenly a noise re-

"TITANIC'S" MILLIONAIRES.

Upon the vessel were men known to have represented a capital of at least £120,000,000. The fortunes of some of these passengers who were lost are given as follows:—

Colonel J. J. Astor	£30,000,000
Mr. B. Guggenheim	20,000,000
Mr. J. Straus	10,000,000
Mr. G. Widener	10,000,000
Mr. W. Roebling	5,000,000
Mr. Charles M. Hays	1,500,000
Mr. William Dulles	1,000,000
Mr. Emil Taussig	1,000,000
Mr. Frederick M. Hoyt	1,000,000
Mr. Clarence Moore	1,000,000

DEATH THE DIVIDER.

As the lifeboats pulled away from the sinking liner there were many sad partings. These included:—

LOST.	SAVED.
Colonel J. J. Astor.	Mrs. Astor.
Mr. Penasco.	Mrs. Penasco.
Mr. J. B. Thayer & Mr. Thayer, jun.	Mrs. J. B Thayer.
Mr. George Widener.	Mrs. G. Widener.
Mr., Mrs. and Miss Allison.	Baby Allison.
Mr. D. W. Marvin.	Mrs. D. W. Marvin.
Mr. C. M. Hays.	Mrs. and Miss Hays.
Mr. Hart.	Mrs. Esther Hart and Child.
Mr. Jacques Futrelle.	Mrs. Jacques Futrelle.
Mr. and Mrs. Wick.	Miss Mary Wick.
Mr. E. C. Crosby.	Mrs. and Miss Crosby.
Mr. T. W. Cavendish.	Mrs. T. W. Cavendish.
Dr. W. E. Minahan.	Mrs. W. E. and Miss D. Minahan.
Mr. E. J. Meyer.	Mrs. E. J. Meyer.
Mr. H. F. Chaffee.	Mrs. H. F. Chaffee.
Mr. W. M. Clarke.	Mrs. W. M. Clarke.
Mr. Thornton Davidson.	Mrs. Thornton Davidson.

THE SHOCK OF DOOM.

O Holy Spirit, Who didst brood
Upon the waters dark and rude,
And bid their angry tumult cease,
And give, for wild confusion, peace;
O hear us when we cry to Thee
For those in peril on the sea.

From ten o'clock there had been on the bridge First Officer Murdock, Fourth Officer Boxall, and Sixth Officer Moody. In the crow's nest were Fleet and another man whose name has not been given. At the wheel was Robert Hichens, one of the quartermasters of the "Titanic."

"At 11.40," says Hichens, "three gongs were sounded from the crow's nest. It was a signal for something right ahead. At the same time one of the men in the nest telephoned that there was a large iceberg ahead."

That was the first message of fate. Down below there was a sleeping population, and some passengers still awake. They knew nothing even then of that approach of death. But by the sound of the three gongs and the message whispered through the telephone the officers at last were startled out of their security. In one swift, blinding flash their deadly peril was revealed. The finger of the Unseen Hand had touched the "Titanic."

"As Officer Murdock's hand was on the lever to stop the engines," says Robert Hichens, "the crash came." He stopped the engines, and then immediately by another lever closed the water-tight doors. Captain Smith came from the chart-room on to the bridge. His first words were—

"Close the emergency doors."

"They are already closed, sir," said Mr. Murdock.

From that moment the tragic figure of Captain Smith stands out clear and defined throughout the awful drama that followed his appearance upon the bridge. He had left his officers of the watch at their post for a little well-earned rest, and he had been recalled by the noise of that shock which told to his trained ears the tale of disaster. Not for a moment could he

sounded like that of the screw when it emerges from the water. We looked at each other in alarm, as we were under the impression that a serious accident had occurred, but we did not then dream of a catastrophe. Ice could be seen through the portholes on the sides of the liner, and the next moment we were all on deck. The 'Titanic' was leaning over on one side."

Among those who had been startled was Mr. Beesley, formerly a master of Dulwich College. His narrative stands as the most clear and coherent description of the great tragedy from first to last:—

"I had been in my berth about ten minutes when, at about 10.15, I felt a slight jar. Then soon afterwards there was a second shock, but it was not sufficiently large to cause any anxiety to anyone, however nervous they may have been. The engines, however, stopped immediately afterwards.

"At first I thought that the ship had lost a propeller. I went up on deck in my dressing gown, and I found only a few people there, who had come up in the same way to inquire why we had stopped; but there was no sort of anxiety in the mind of anyone.

"We saw through the smoking-room window that a game of cards was going on, and I went in to ask if they knew anything. They had noticed the jar a little more, and, looking through the window, had seen a huge iceberg go by close to the side of the boat. They thought that we had just grazed it with a glancing blow, and they had been to see if any damage had been done.

"None of us, of course, had any conception that the ship had been pierced below by part of a submerged iceberg.

"The game of cards was resumed, and without any thought of disaster I retired to my cabin to read until we started again. I never saw any of the players or the onlookers again.

"A little later, hearing people going upstairs, I went out again, and found that everybody wanted to know why the engines had stopped. No doubt many of them had been awakened from their sleep by the sudden stopping of the vibration to which they had become accustomed during the four days we had been on board.

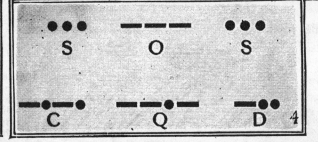

SOME FACTS OF THE DISASTER.

The iceberg, from 50 to 100 feet high, was struck at 11.35 p.m.

The blow was a glancing one on the starboard side, which was ripped open, rendering useless the essential water-tight compartments.

The "Titanic" sank in two miles of water, two hours and forty-five minutes after she struck.

Jack Phillips, the "Titanic's" wireless operator, remained at his post flashing out signals for assistance until the deck was awash.

Captain Smith, indifferent to his own safety, worked till the very last moment to save as many as possible. "Be British" was his word to one and all.

The "Carpathia's" wireless operator, by a lucky chance, was up late, and heard the "Titanic's" call for help.

The White Star liner "Olympic," on hearing the "Titanic's" wireless call for assistance, covered 400 miles at twenty-four knots, the highest speed the liner has ever attained.

How the wireless call for help was sent.

(1.) Jack Phillips, the chief Marconi operator on the "Titanic," who flashed out his messages till the ship went down.

(2.) The wireless cabin on an ocean liner, the operator receiving a message.

(3.) Harold Bride, the second Marconi operator on the "Titanic," who was saved.

(4.) The wireless signal of distress, "S. O. S." in the Morse code. Formerly the signal "C. Q. D." was used.

"Going up on the deck again, I saw that there was an unmistakable list downwards from the stern to the bows, but knowing nothing of what had happened I concluded that some of the front compartments had filled and had weighed her down.

"Again I went down to my cabin, where I put on some warmer clothing. As I dressed I heard the order shouted, 'All the passengers on deck with lifebelts on.'"

Before this order was given Captain Smith had gone to the "wireless" room. He had ascertained by that time that the damage to the "Titanic" was very grave, and that, in spite of all her water-tight compartments, she was filling rapidly. There was but one thing to do: to call for help across the sea in the hope that the appeal might be heard and answered by ships within reach of those wireless words. Never before had Captain Smith sent such a message out into the darkness. But now he must make use of that modern miracle invented by Marconi, by which ships may speak across the great silence of the sea.

There were two men in the wireless cabin—Phillips, the first operator, and Bride, the second operator. It was but a little room, yet large enough for heroic virtues. And Phillips was a hero great as any on the roll-call of honour. His name is imperishable; his death a glorious tradition. As will be seen later in this narrative, he did his duty to the uttermost and with a sublime devotion, careless of death. The story of his heroism and of all that happened in that wireless cabin has been told by Harold Bride, who shares the honour of his comrade:—

"On the night of the accident I was not 'sending,' but was asleep. There were three rooms in the wireless cabin: one was the sleeping room, one the dynamo room, and the other the operating room.

"I took off my clothes and went to sleep in bed. I was conscious of waking up and hearing Phillips sending to Cape Race. I read what he sent; it was traffic matter. I remembered how tired he was, and got out of bed without my clothes on to relieve him.

"I did not even feel a shock. I hardly knew anything had happened. I was standing by Phillips telling him to go to bed when the captain put his head in the cabin.

"'We've struck an iceberg,' he said, 'and I'm having an inspection made to tell what it's done to us. You'd better get ready to send out a call for assistance; but don't send it until I tell you.'

"The captain went away, but in ten minutes, I estimate, he came back. We could hear some confusion outside, but there was not the least thing to indicate that there was any trouble. The wireless was working perfectly.

"'Send a call for assistance,' ordered the captain, barely putting his head in the door.

"'What call should I send?' Phillips asked.

"'The regulation international call for help, just that.' Then the captain was gone.

"Phillips began to send the 'C.Q.D.' (the old signal, now replaced by 'S.O.S.'). He flashed away at it. We joked while he did so. All of us made light of the disaster. We joked that way while he flashed signals for about five minutes. Then the captain came back.

"'What are you sending?' he asked. 'C.Q.D.' Phillips replied.

"The humour of the situation appealed to me. I cut in with a little remark that made us all laugh, including the captain. 'Send S.O.S.,' I said; 'it's the new call. It may be your last chance.' Phillips, with a laugh, changed the signal to 'S.O.S.'

"The captain told us we had been struck amidships or just back of amidships. It was ten minutes, Phillips told me, after he had noticed a slight jolt. That was the only signal to us that a collision had occured.

"In the next few minutes we picked up the first steamship, the 'Frankfurt.' We gave her our position, and said we had struck an iceberg and needed assistance. The 'Frankfurt's' operator went away to tell his captain. When he came back we told him we were sinking by the head. By that time we could observe a distinct list forward.

"The 'Carpathia' answered our signal. We told her our position and said we were sinking by the head. The operator went to tell his captain, and five minutes after returned and told us the 'Carpathia' was putting about and heading for us. Our captain had left us at this time, and Phillips said to me, 'Run and tell him what the "Carpathia" has answered.' I did so, and went through an awful mass of people to his cabin.

"I came back and heard Phillips giving the 'Carpathia' fuller directions. Phillips told me to put on my clothes. Until that moment I had forgotten I was not dressed.

"I went to my cabin and dressed. I brought an overcoat to Phillips; it was very cold, and I slipped the coat upon him while he worked.

"Every few minutes Phillips would send me to the captain with little messages, merely telling how the 'Carpathia' was coming our way, and giving her speed. I noticed as I came back from one trip that they were putting off the women and children in lifeboats."

THE OLD RULE OF THE SEA.

They shall not say in England that we fought
With shameful strength unhonoured life to seek,
Into mean safety, mean deserters, bought
By trampling down the weak.

So we made women with their children go,
The oars ply back again, and yet again;
Whilst, inch by inch, the drowning ship sank low
Still under steadfast men.

It was to Mr. Lightoller, the second officer, that Captain Smith gave his last recorded order from the bridge:—

"Put the women and children into the boats, and lower away."

In that one sentence there was a world of woe. In the captain's soul there was the terrible admission that this immense vessel, which had been called "unsinkable," was sinking; that it would be safer for human lives to be out on the sea of night in small boats than upon the ship which still towered up like an impregnable fortress of steel, whose lights were still brilliant along her tiers of decks, whose power still seemed prodigious and complete. The captain's order was the confession of an enormous tragedy.

The meaning of it was not yet clear to all those people who now crowded the decks. They were startled, dazed, full of a wondering perplexity, but not panic-stricken. They were conscious of a sudden peril that had lurched out upon them from the darkness, but they did not understand its full and dreadful significance. They could not believe that the "Titanic" had been struck a mortal blow. Something had gone wrong. Some iceberg had been struck. The officers were taking the proper precautions as a matter of form. It was a great nuisance. It put a strain upon one's nerves to be called like this from one's sleep to stand insufficiently clad in the intense cold of the night air. Surely it could mean nothing worse than that? Oh, God! it could not mean anything worse?... So in those first moments of alarm did the people of the "Titanic" stifle their vague fear and maintain their quietude.

The captain came down on deck. "He was munching a toothpick," said one of the three French witnesses. He was master of himself. To the people who called out questions to him he said, "Everyone must put on his lifebelt. It is more prudent to do so."

The orders were called along the corridors of the sleeping decks, and people obeyed reluctantly, though many remained, it seems, in their cabins. Mr. Beesley, the former master of Dulwich, continues his story:—

"We all walked up slowly with the lifebelts tied on over our clothing, but even then we presumed that this was merely a wise precaution the captain was taking, and that we should return in a short time to go to bed. There was a total absence of any panic or expression of alarm. I suppose this must be accounted for by the exceeding calmness of the night and the absence of any signs of an accident.

"The ship was absolutely still, and, except for the gentle tilt downwards, which I don't think one person in ten would have noticed at the time, there were no visible signs of the approaching disaster. She lay just as if waiting for the order to go on again when some trifling matter had been adjusted.

"In a few moments, however, we saw the covers being lifted from the boats, and the crews allotted to them standing by and uncoiling the ropes which were to lower them. We then began to realise that it was a more serious matter than we had at first supposed.

"My first thought was to go down to get more clothing and some money, but, seeing people pouring up the stairs, I decided that it was better to cause no confusion to people coming up by attempting to get to my cabin.

"Presently we heard the order, 'All men stand back away from the boats. All ladies retire to the next deck below,' which was the smoking-room or B deck.

Loading the Lifeboats.

Captain Smith had gone to the bridge again. According to Robert Hichens, the man at the wheel, "the skipper" looked at the commutator, which showed in what direction the ship was listing. She appeared to carry a five-degree list to starboard. The ship was then rapidly settling forward, and all the steam sirens were blowing. By the captain's order the engines were then put to work pumping out the ship. Rockets were sent up from the bridge by Lowe, the fifth mate, and all hands were ordered on deck. Lifebelts were served out to the crew, and the stewards and other hands helped the sailors in getting the boats out. That seemed to have taken some time. Forty-five minutes had passed since the signal from the crow's nest before Second Officer Lightoller ordered Hichens away from the wheel, and told him to take charge of one of the boats and load it with women. It was then 12.25 a.m. Out of the darkness came an officer's voice:

"Women and children first!"

It was only then that it began to dawn upon the passengers that they were indeed threatened by a terrible calamity. It was only then that many of them realised with an awful anguish that husbands were to be separated from wives, and all men from all women, according to the old law of the sea in time of shipwreck, according to what Second Officer Lightoller called "the law of human nature." Oh, terrible law, for women to be taken away from those they loved best in the world! Oh, tragic law, for men who could no longer protect their wives and daughters, their young brides, their own mothers, from the perils of death! Oh, law of tragic farewells and awful separation!

It was now that the great agony began on the ship of doom. It was now that all the courage in men's hearts was put to the great test, and now that the love of women was torn and bleeding, and now that all the temptation of fear, of cowardice, of selfish despair, which assail human nature when death looks it in its eyes and beckons must have tried their utmost to gain the master hand. But in nearly every case men strangled their fear and drowned the dem ~f temptation swiftly; and women, frail and delicate, nurtured in luxury, rose above their weakness, and obtained by a kind of miracle unflinching courage.

The drama of heroism began. There were many noble actors upon that dark stage of the death-ship. The figures flit to and fro. One sees them only in swift flashes before they disappear for ever. But every little act which was revealed momentarily on those decks shines with the bright light of self-sacrifice, of chivalry, of noble dignity.

The women were gathered there, some lightly clad, some who had taken leisure to dress, and the men, who understood more clearly than many of these ladies the real significance of what was taking place, soothed them with reassuring words, and tried to hide from them the horror of the scene.

The ship's band, conducted by Mr. Hartley, whose name will be remembered always as one of the greatest heroes of

Some well-known passengers who went down on the "Titanic" :—

1. Senator Carter
2. Mr. W. T. Stead
3 & 4. Mr. & Mrs. Strauss
5. Major Archibald Butt
6. Colonel J. J. Astor
7. Mr. C. M. Hayes
8. Senator Allison
9. Mr. T. W. Cavendish
10. Mr. Benjamin Guggenheim

the "Titanic," assembled on one of the decks, and while the boats were being lowered played selections from operas and the latest popular melodies. That merry music floating out above the quiet waters under the star-strewn sky set the keynote to this great melody of spiritual devotion to honour and duty. Let us look now at some of the single figures in this deadly drama.

There was Colonel Astor, the American millionaire, who was returning from his honeymoon. He had given a helping hand with the boats; he had spoken words of courage and good cheer to those who seemed frightened. Then he stood for a moment by the side of his beautiful bride. Mr. Edward Wheelton, chief steward of the "Titanic," watched him at that moment.

"I heard Colonel Astor tell his wife that he would meet her in New York. They exchanged an affectionate farewell, but no more affectionate than that of a couple separating just for a week instead of eternity."

As the boats with the women went away from the side of the ship Colonel Astor stood for a moment at the salute. He called out a last farewell to his wife: "Good-bye, dearie, I will join you later." Then he turned calmly and lit a cigarette, and leaned over the rails, staring through the darkness.

Major Butt, President Taft's aide-de-camp, had been close to Colonel Astor and had behaved with a chivalry and the quiet cheerful courage of a gallant gentleman.

"He was very calm," says Mr. Wheelton, the steward. "He gave his orders coolly and pacified men who were inclined to be panicky. I last saw him standing by the rail looking into the water."

Miss Marie Young, of Washington, formerly a teacher of music to the children of President Roosevelt, was the last person to bid Major Butt good-bye.

"I was on the last boat," she says, "that put off from the 'Titanic.' I knew Major Butt in Washington, and we resumed our acquaintance on the 'Titanic.' He was so cool and collected that he inspired all who came in contact with him with courage. He helped me to my seat in the lifeboat as coolly as if he were handing me to a chair in a drawing-room, and when the boat was lowered he stood on the deck, and, taking off his hat, said 'Good-bye,' and smilingly waved his hand to me. He stood upon the watery deck as our boat pulled off, and the very last I saw of this brave man was while he stood there waving his hat and smiling."

One of the stewards who was instrumental in getting the people away in the boats says that Mr. Benjamin Guggenheim, the New York banker, was offered a place in one of the lifeboats, but he refused, saying, "I will not go. No woman shall remain unsaved because I was a coward." Mr. Guggenheim gave the steward, whose name is Etches, a message for his wife, which was afterwards delivered.

"If I don't turn up," he said, "tell my wife that I have done the best I could."

He was one of those who went down.

But he and a friend found time to return to their cabins and put on evening dress. When the steward expressed his amazement Mr. Guggenheim smiled and said, "If we have to die we will die like gentlemen," It was the same spirit in which Lord Nelson put on his medals and stars before the battle of Trafalgar.

A noble story of a woman's sacrifice was told by one of the survivors :—

"We were about to put off in a lifeboat," she said, "every seat being taken, all by women. Miss Edith Evans, one of the first-cabin passengers, had taken her place in the boat when she suddenly discovered that her aunt was left on the deck of the sinking liner.

"Miss Evans immediately got out of the boat, and insisted on giving up her place to her aunt. 'I am not married,' said she, 'and my loss makes no difference, but you have children, and you must go to them.'

"With some difficulty she persuaded her aunt to take her place, and this brave woman, whose name ought to be remembered, remained on the vessel and sank with her."

Mr. Henry Harris, the New York theatrical manager, made an historic answer to an old command. When the first boats were being filled—without haste, because the danger did not

arms of the men and throw them over the side into the boats."

Mr. Lowe, the fifth mate, in giving evidence before the American Senate, said :—

"First it was a case of only women and children, and after that a few men got away, but they went irrespective of rank or class." One Italian on his boat escaped from the 'Titanic' disguised as a woman. He had a shawl around him. "I just picked him up in my arms," said Mr. Lowe, a stalwart man, "and pitched him into another lifeboat not so heavily laden as ours."

With regard to his boat there seems to have been some little trouble, and Mr. Lowe fired a few shots into the air as a warning to some Italians among the steerage passengers on the lower decks.

"One more body falling into our boat," continued Mr. Lowe, "as we lowered, might have buckled up our boat. I knew the risk we ran, and I feared that, as we came down to the water, some people might make a rush from the lower decks, jumping the intervening 3 ft. between the ship's side and the lifeboat, and so cause a disaster. I was in lifeboat 14, and, in my judgment, had as many as we could carry. I expected every moment my boat would double up under my feet as we descended, and I feared more weight. I saw the Italian and Latin people on the lower decks as we came down, all glaring and ready to spring, and, as I holloaed, 'Look out!' I let bang just along the ship's side, between our boat and the 'Titanic.' I hurt nobody; I fired into space."

Even now there were many women who refused to go with the boats because they believed there was greater safety on the vessel, and many men who refused to believe that the

THE LOST AND SAVED.

The following figures, issued by the Board of Trade, give full official details of the lost and saved among the passengers and crew of the "Titanic."

	First Class.			Second Class.			Third Class.			Total Passengers.			Crew.			Total Passengers and Crew.		
	Carried	Saved	Per Cent. Saved	Carried	Saved	Per Cent. Saved	Carried	Saved	Per Cent. Saved	Carried	Saved	Per Cent. Saved	Carried	Saved	Per Cent. Saved	Carried	Saved	Per Cent. Saved
Men ...	173	58	34	160	13	8	454	55	12	787	126	16	875	189	22	1,662	315	19
Women	144	139	97	93	78	84	179	98	55	416	315	76	23	21	91	439	336	77
Children	5	5	100	24	24	100	76	23	30	105	52	49	—	—	—	105	52	49
Total ...	322	202	63	277	115	42	709	176	25	1,308	493	38	898	210	23	2,206	703	32

seem imminent—Mr. Harris took his place in a boat by the side of his wife. "Women first," said one of the ship's officers in charge of the embarkation. "Certainly," said Mr. Harris, as he kissed his wife, pressed her for a moment to his breast, and then climbed back to the "Titanic." That "Certainly" was a brave word.

Mr. Stead, Mr. Howard Case, and the American novelist, Mr. Jacques Futrelle, were conspicuous for their fine conduct, assisting the women and children in the boats. All remained to perish.

Heroic was the behaviour of the great merchant, Mr. Isidor Straus. When urged to save himself he exclaimed, "Not as long as a single woman remains on board."

Sailors tried to force Mrs. Straus into a boat. She was an old lady, but she clung to her husband with desperate strength.

"I will stay where you are!" she cried to him. "We have lived for forty years together, and will not part now in old age." This Darby and Joan of America sank in each other's arms as the "Titanic" plunged to death.

There were many other women who refused to leave their husbands, and many who were forced weeping from their husbands' arms by sailors who insisted upon them getting into the boats.

It seems beyond doubt that there was some confusion in the loading of the boats.

"I learned later," says Mr. Daniel, a banker of Philadelphia, "that there was a conflict of orders given. When the boats were filled on the starboard side, husbands were ordered to enter the smaller craft with their wives on the port side. The husbands were then driven back, the order being 'Women and children first.' In many instances within the range of my vision wives refused point blank to leave their husbands. I saw members of the crew literally pull the women from the

great ship was doomed. They had a pitiful faith in the unsinkable strength of the "Titanic." It is for this reason that some of the boats went away without a full load of passengers. A vivid narrative of what happened in the case of one boat is given by Mr. Beesley, from whose story we have already quoted. It continues from the point when the first order was given for the boats to be lowered.

"The men all stood away, and waited in absolute silence, some leaning against the end railings of the deck, others pacing slowly up and down. The boats were then swung out and lowered from A deck. When they were level with B deck, where all the women were collected, the women got in quietly with the exception of some who refused to leave their husbands.

"In some cases they were torn from their husbands and pushed into the boats, but in many instances they were allowed to remain, since there was no one to insist that they should go.

"Looking over the side, one saw the boats from aft already in the water slipping quietly away into the darkness. Presently the boats near me were lowered with much creaking, as the new ropes slipped through the pulleys and blocks down the 90 ft. which separated them from the water.

"An officer in uniform came up as one boat went down, and shouted out, 'When you're afloat, row round to the companion ladder and stand by with other boats for orders.'

"'Aye, aye, sir,' came the reply, but I don't think any boat was able to obey the order, for when they were afloat and had their oars at work the condition of the rapidly settling liner was much more apparent. In common prudence the sailors saw that they could do nothing but row from the sinking ship, and so save at any rate some lives. They, no doubt, anticipated that the suction from such an enormous vessel would be more than usually dangerous to the crowded boat, which was mostly filled with women.

[By courtesy of "The Sphere."

Special drawing to show the relative position of the "Titanic" and other liners on the icefield. The "Carpathia," which picked up the survivors, raced to the rescue from the westward.

" All this time there was no trace of any disorder. There was no panic or rush to the boats, and there were no scenes of women sobbing hysterically, such as one generally pictures happening at such times. Everyone seemed to realise so slowly that there was imminent danger, that, when it was realised that we might all be presently in the sea, with nothing but our lifebelts to support us until we were picked up by passing steamers, it was extraordinary how calm everyone was, how completely self-controlled we were as one by one the boats filled with women and children were lowered and rowed away into the night.

" Presently word went round among us that men were to be put in boats on the starboard side. I was on the port side. Most of the men walked across the deck to see if this was true. I remained where I was, and shortly afterwards I heard the call, ' Any more ladies?' Looking over the side of the ship, I saw boat No. 13 swinging level with ' B ' deck. It was half-full of women. Again the call was repeated, ' Any more ladies?' I saw none coming. Then one of the crew looked up and said, ' Any ladies on your deck, sir?' ' No,' I replied.

" ' Then you'd better jump,' said he. I dropped and fell into the bottom of the boat as they cried ' Lower away!'

" As the boat began to descend two ladies were pushed hurriedly through the crowd on ' B ' deck, and a baby ten months old was passed down after them. Then down we went, the crew shouting out directions to those lowering us. ' Level,' ' Aft,' ' Stern,' ' Both together,' until we were some 10 ft. from the water. Here occurred the only anxious moment we had during the whole of our experience from the time of our leaving the deck to our reaching the ' Carpathia.'

" Immediately below our boat was the exhaust of the condensers, and a huge stream of water was pouring all the time from the ship's side just above the water-line. It was plain that we ought to be smart away from it if we were to escape swamping when we touched the water.

" We had no officers on board, and no petty officer or member of the crew to take charge, so one of the stokers shouted, ' Someone find the pin which releases the boat from the ropes, and pull it up!' No one knew where it was. We felt as well as we could on the floor and along the sides, but found nothing.

It was difficult to move among so many people. We had sixty or seventy on board. Down we went, and presently we floated, with our ropes still holding us, and the stream of water from the exhaust washing us away from the side of the vessel, while the swell of the sea urged us back against the side again.

" The resultant of all these forces was that we were carried parallel to the ship's side and directly under boat No. 14, which had filled rapidly and was coming down on us in a way that threatened to submerge our boat.

" ' Stop lowering 14,' our crew shouted, and the crew of No. 14, now only 20 ft. above, cried out the same. The distance to the top, however, was some 70 ft., and the creaking of the pulleys must have deadened all sound to those above, for down she came, 15 ft., 10 ft., 5 ft., and a stoker and I reached up and touched the bottom of the swinging boat above our heads.

" The next drop would have brought her on our heads. Just before she dropped another stoker sprang to the ropes with his knife open in his hand. ' One,' I heard him say, and then ' Two,' as the knife cut through the pulley rope.

" The next moment the exhaust stream carried us clear, while boat No. 14 dropped into the water. Our gunwales were almost touching. We drifted away easily, and when our oars were got out we headed directly away from the ship."

There was one tragic figure on the ship who went up and down the decks, hiding his despair by helping the women to the boats. It was Mr. Bruce Ismay, the general manager of the White Star Line. He had seen the building of the ship since the keel was laid. He was one of her owners. He had been proud of this latest and grandest achievement of naval architecture. He had come in to watch her conduct upon the maiden voyage, confident in her power, sure of her triumphant progress across the Atlantic. Now all his pride was abased, all his confidence scattered by that stab in the dark which had ripped up the grand keel and destroyed all the devices which had been designed for keeping her watertight. As he was on one of the lower decks the last boat was being filled, and the officers called out to know if there were any more women to go. No woman answered, and there were no passengers on the deck. As the boat was lowered away Mr. Ismay got into it, as other men, like Mr. Beesley, had got into other boats for the same reason.

THE LAST SCENES ON THE SINKING SHIP.

Nothing is here for tears, nothing to wail,
Or knock the breast, no weakness, no contempt,
Dispraise or blame, nothing but well and fair,
And what may quiet us in a death so noble.

The last lifeboat pulled away and disappeared into the darkness; and on the "Titanic" there remained more than 1,600 human beings face to face with death. In a little while they knew that death was very close to them. They could hear its voice calling to them. Their souls stared into eternity. Yet even now there were men and women who buoyed themselves up with hope, according to that divine law of life by which hope is only abandoned in the arms of death. Even now some of them clung with faith to the "Titanic's" enduring strength. But that hope and that faith were not strong enough to hide the dreadful possibility. It was the hope of condemned men waiting for a reprieve at the eleventh hour.

The "Titanic" was sinking by the head. The water was rising in her great hold. If there was to be a rescue it must come quickly.

But still there was no panic.

"There were no lamentations," said Mr. Lightoller, "and no demonstration, either from the men or the passengers as they saw the last lifeboat go, and there was no wailing, no crying, no outburst from the men who lined the ship's rail as she disappeared from sight."

"The men," he said, "stood as quietly as if they were in church."

The greatest hope of help, if there were any hope worth clinging to, lay in the wireless cabin. From that little room messages were still throbbing across the sea, calling, calling, calling to any ship that might be passing in the night. As we know now, those cries for help were heard by several ships and answered. Let us go again into the wireless room and continue the story told by Harold Bride, with Phillips as the hero:—

"I noticed that the list forward was increasing. Phillips told me the wireless was growing weaker, and the captain came and informed us that our engine-rooms were taking in water, and that the dynamos might not last much longer. We sent those facts to the 'Carpathia.'

"Every man for himself."

"I went out on deck and looked around. The water was close up to the boat deck. There was a great scramble aft, and how poor Phillips worked through it I don't know.

"He was a brave man. I learned to love him that night, for I suddenly felt for him a great reverence, seeing him standing there sticking to his work while everybody else was raging about. I will never forget the work of Phillips in the last awful fifteen minutes.

"I thought it was about time to look about to see if there was anything detached that would float. I remembered that every member of the crew had a special lifebelt and ought to know where it was. I remembered that mine was under the bunk and went and got it. Then I thought how cold the water was, and I put my boots and an extra jacket on.

"I saw Phillips standing out there still sending away, giving the 'Carpathia' details just how we were doing.

"We picked up the 'Olympic' and told her we were sinking by the head.

"'We're about all down.' As Phillips was sending that message I strapped his lifebelt to his back. I had already put on his overcoat, and I wondered if I could get him into his boots. He suggested with a sort of laugh that I should look out and see if all the people were off in the boats, or if any boats were left, or how things were.

"I saw a collapsible boat near the funnel and went over to it. Twelve men were trying to boost it down to the boat deck. They were having an awful time. It was the last boat left. I looked at it longingly for a few minutes, then I gave them a hand. Over she went, and they all started to scramble in.

"I walked back to Phillips and said, 'The last raft is gone.' Then came the captain's voice:

"'Men, you have done your full duty. You can do no more. Abandon your cabin now. It's every man for himself. You look out for yourselves. I release you—that's the way of it at this kind of time, every man for himself.'

"I looked out. The boat deck was awash. Phillips clung on . . . sending . . . sending. He clung on for about ten minutes, or maybe fifteen minutes, after the captain released him. The water was then coming into our cabin while he worked.

"Something happened now that I hate to tell about. I was back in my room getting Phillips's money for him. As I looked out of the door I saw a stoker or somebody from below decks leaning over Phillips from behind. Phillips was too busy to notice what the man was doing. He was slipping the lifebelt off Phillips's back.

"He was a big man, too, and, as you can see, I am very small. I don't know what it was I got hold of. I remembered in a flash the way Phillips had clung on; how I had to fix that lifebelt in place because he was too busy to do it.

"I knew that the man from below decks had his own lifebelt and should have known where to get it. I suddenly felt a passion not to let that man die a decent sailor's death. I wished he might have stretched a rope or walked the plank. I did my duty. . . . I hope I finished him; I don't know. We left him on the cabin floor of the wireless room, and he wasn't moving.

"From aft came the tunes of the band. There was a ragtime tune, I don't know what, and then there was "Autumn" (used as a recessional in America).

"Phillips ran aft, and that was the last I saw of him. I went to the place where I had seen a collapsible boat on the boat deck. A large wave came awash of the deck and carried the boat off.

"I had hold of an oarlock. I went off with it, and the next I knew I was in the boat. But that wasn't all. I was in the boat, and the boat was upside down, I under it.

"I remember realising that I was wet through, and that, whatever happened, I must breathe. I knew I had to fight for it, and did. How I got out from under the boat I don't know, but I felt a breath of air at last."

Besides calling to the "Carpathia" and the "Olympic," Phillips had also spoken to the "Baltic" and the "Frankfurt," and from the wireless station at Cape Race other vessels had been sent to the rescue. But they were all very far away, and though they made all speed towards the doomed ship, not one of them was near when the last dread moment came.

Water was now flooding the upper decks. Second Officer Lightoller was up to the ankles in water. Captain Smith stood on the bridge, a calm, grave figure, conscious that the end was near. Two words came down from him to the people who were crowding forward:

"Be British!"

It was a call to the old traditions of our race and manhood. The band was still playing. They played until they were waist high in water. In that dread moment Hartley, the conductor, spoke to his comrades, and there throbbed out into the darkness, heard by the women in the boats far away, the hymn of faith and pleading, which went up to the Eternal Father.

THE LAST HYMN.

Nearer, my God, to thee,
Nearer to thee!
E'en though it be a cross
That raiseth me:
Still all my song shall be,
"Nearer, my God, to thee—
Nearer to thee!"

Though, like the wanderer,
The sun gone down,
Darkness be over me,
My rest a stone;
Yet in my dreams I'd be
Nearer, my God, to thee,
Nearer to thee!

There let the way appear,
Steps unto heaven;
All that thou send'st to me
In mercy given,
Angels to beckon me
Nearer, my God, to thee,
Nearer to thee!

Suddenly there was the noise of a great explosion. Down below, where the engineers and stokers still stood at their posts, the boilers burst as the water flooded into their chambers. It was the signal of death. The "Titanic" was broken in two. Her mighty stern rose clear out of the water, and stayed for a little while pointing like a black finger of fate through the darkness. Then her head went down, and very quietly, without great turbulence of waters, the vast ship dived down into the dark sea and disappeared for ever from the sight of men. The greatest tragedy in the story of the sea had been accomplished. Humanity had received its greatest shock. God welcomed many souls that night.

"NEARER, MY GOD, TO THEE,"
the hymn played by the band of the "Titanic" as she sank. The portrait is that of Mr. W. Hartley, the bandmaster.

4. Then, with my waking thoughts,
   Bright with Thy praise
   Out of my stony griefs
   Bethel I'll raise;
   So by my woes to be
   Nearer, my God, to Thee,
   — Nearer to Thee.

5. Or if on joyful wing
   Cleaving the sky
   Sun, moon and stars forgot
   Upwards I fly.
   Still all my song shall be
   Nearer, my God, to Thee,
   Nearer to Thee.

THE HEROIC MUSICIANS.

The brave bandsmen who played "Nearer, my God, to Thee" while the "Titanic" was sinking fast were:—

W. HARTLEY (Bandmaster),
Surreyside,
West Park Street,
Dewsbury.

J. HUME,
George Street,
Dumfries.

P. C. TAYLOR,
Fentiman Road,
Clapham,
London.

J. W. WOODWARD,
The Firs,
Windmill Road,
Headington,
Oxon.

R. BRICOUX,
Place du Lion d'Or,
Lille,
France.

. CLARKE,
Tunstall Street,
Smithdown Road,
Liverpool.

G. KRIUS,
Villa Road,
Brixton,
London.

W. T. BRAILEY,
Lancaster Road,
Ladbroke Grove,
London.

IN THE WATERS OF DEATH.

Ships that pass in the night, and speak each other in passing;
Only a signal shown, and a distant voice in the darkness.
So, on the ocean of life we pass and speak one another:
Only a look and a voice, then darkness again, and silence.

A great chorus of human agony, a great and bitter cry, went wailing up to the black dome of night as 1,600 human beings or more plunged into the sea of death. The story of what followed is agonising, yet must be told, because out of its horror there shines the most heroic virtue, and the victory of death was greater than its tragedy. It has been told by those who escaped in a miraculous manner.

Mr. Lightoller, the second officer, is one of those who lived to tell the story.

"I was standing on the top of the officers' quarters," he said. "There was nothing more to be done. The last boat had been sent away . . . the ship took a dive . . . I faced forward and also took a dive."

He was sucked to the side of the ship against the grating over the blower for the exhaust. There was an explosion, and it blew him to the surface of the water again, only to be sucked back once more by the water rushing into the ship. This time he landed against the grating over the pipes which furnish the draught for the funnels and stuck there. There was another explosion, and again he came to the surface not many feet from the ship, and on the other side of her, before she made her final plunge. He came up near a capsized collapsible boat and clung to it. A funnel fell within four inches of him and

killed many swimmers. Thirty clung to the capsized boat and a lifeboat with forty survivors in it already finally took him off.

There were other escapes as miraculous apparently as this. Mr. Whiteman, the "Titanic's" barber, was blown off the deck by the second of two explosions in the boilers. A bundle of deck-chairs roped together was blown off the deck with him and struck his back, injuring his spine, but serving as a raft until he was picked up two hours later.

Mr. J. B. Thayer, jun., son of the president of the Pennsylvania Railway, was swept down with the boat as she sank, and then hurled into the air "by some extraordinary force," and later was picked up alive and saved by one of the boats.

The scene of the "Titanic's" last moments, and of the human agony that followed, was watched by those who had escaped in the boats, and described afterwards in haunting words.

"It was one o'clock in the morning," says Mr. Beesley, continuing his narrative. "The starlight night was beautiful, but as there was no moon it was not very light. The sea was as calm as a pond. There was just a gentle heave as the boat dipped up and down in the swell. It was an ideal night, except for the bitter cold.

"In the distance the 'Titanic' looked enormous. Her length and her great bulk were outlined in black against the starry sky. Every porthole and saloon was blazing with light. It was impossible to think that anything could be wrong with such a leviathan were it not for that ominous tilt downward in the bows, where the water was by now up to the lowest row of portholes.

"At about two o'clock we observed her settling very rapidly, with the bows and the bridge completely under water. She slowly tilted straight on end with the stern vertically upwards. As she did so the lights in the cabins and the saloons, which had not flickered for a moment since we left, died out, flashed once more, and then went out altogether.

"At the same time the machinery roared down through the vessel with a groaning rattle that could have been heard for miles. It was the weirdest sound, surely, that could have been heard in the middle of the ocean. It was not yet quite the end. To our amazement she remained in that upright position for a time, which I estimate as five minutes.

"It was certainly for some minutes that we watched at least 150 feet of the 'Titanic' towering up above the level of the sea, looming black against the sky. Then with a quiet, slant-ing dive she disappeared beneath the waters. Our eyes had looked for the last time on the gigantic vessel in which we set out from Southampton.

"Then there fell on our ears the most appalling noise that human being ever heard—the cries of hundreds of our fellow-beings struggling in the icy waters, crying for help with a cry that we knew could not be answered. We longed to return to pick up some of those who were swimming, but this would have meant the swamping of our boat and the loss of all of us."

The three Frenchmen who had been playing cards when the crash came also watched the tragic scene from one of the boats.

"Our boat proceeded to a distance of half a mile, and what a fairy-like spectacle did we behold! The 'Titanic,' entirely illuminated, superb in her immobility, appeared in a strange setting. The night was clear and the sea perfectly calm, but the weather was very cold. The huge ship began to go down by the head, and then suddenly the lights went out. A loud cry arose from everyone in a supreme appeal. Little by little

"Beautiful was death in him, who saw the death and kept the deck,
Saving women and their babes, and sinking with the sinking wreck."

The dreadful story of what happened when the "iTtanic" had sank beneath the quiet sea and when hundreds of figures were struggling in the water around the place where she had towered up a little while before will never be fully told. The survivors shrink from telling the full details of that awful story When Mr. Lightoller was asked to describe the scene before the American Senate an expression of poignant caution came from him. In his eyes there was the look of a man who recalls a dreadful vision. "Don't, sir!" he cried to the man who was interrogating him. But we must not hush up the incidents which shewed human virtue in its brightest, noblest aspect. Though they tear at one's heartstrings, they are idylls of heroic self-sacrifice and courage. Mr. Caldwell, a second-class passen-ger who leaped into the water just before the liner sank, tells one of these beautiful deeds.

He swam about for nearly an hour, and was stricken with despair by the presence of a number of dead bodies about him, floating by means of life-belts. He swam cheek by jowl with Death.

He was about to give up hope when he found himself near a crate, which was supporting another man.

"'Will it hold two?' I asked," says Mr. Caldwell.

"The other man replied, 'Catch on; we'll try. We will live or die together.'

"We finally reached an overturned lifeboat, which had six seamen holding on to the bottom. When we had crawled on to the keel the boat in her capsized condition was carrying all

---

THE KING'S MESSAGE TO THE PRESIDENT.

The King sent the following telegram to the President of the United States on learning of the disaster :—

The Queen and I are anxious to assure you and the American nation of the great sorrow which we experience at the terrible loss of life that has occurred among the American citizens and my own subjects by the foundering of the "Titanic."

Our two countries are so intimately allied by ties of friendship and brotherhood that any misfortune which affects the one must necessarily affect the other, and on the present heartrending occasion they are both equally sufferers.

(Signed) GEORGE R. & I.

THE PRESIDENT'S MESSAGE TO THE KING.

In reply, President Taft sent the following cable to the King :—

In the presence of the appalling disaster to the "Titanic," the people of our two countries are brought into a community of grief through their common bereavement.

The American people share in the sorrow of their kinsmen beyond the sea, and on behalf of my countrymen I thank you for your sympathetic message.

---

the 'Titanic' went lower. The cries of anguish of the unhappy passengers redoubled, sounding like the singing of a dirge, with the most weird persistence, by a very large choir. Some-times there was silence, and then we imagined that the end had come. But no! After a moment the tragic choir broke in again with more emotion, more despair, than before.

"As for us, we thought only of rowing harder than ever to escape those haunting death cries, which wrung our very souls, mingled with the sighing of the sea. They lasted about half an hour, then one by one the voices died away.

"Strange to say, the 'Titanic' foundered almost noiselessly. The suction, contrary to what was expected, was very slight. A great splash, and that was all. The giant of the ocean was no more. In one last spasm the stern reared itself aloft, and then the ship disappeared for ever."

The death of Captain Smith was sublime in its heroism. Faithful to the old tradition of seamanship, he stood upon the bridge until his ship sank below him. A strong swimmer, he remained alive in that ice-cold water, and, as told by Mr. Charles Williams, the racquet coach of Harrow School, who was picked up by one of the lifeboats, the captain's last act was to save a little child.

Soon after Mr. Williams had been hauled into the boat Captain Smith swam up to it, supporting a baby on his left arm and swimming with his right.

"Take the child!" he gasped.

A dozen hands reached forth to grasp the baby, which was taken into the boat. They then tried to pull the captain into the boat, but he refused.

"What became of Murdock?" he asked.

When someone answered that he was dead, "the captain," said Mr. Williams, "released his grasp of the gunwale and slowly sank before our eyes."

she could manage. Presently a man came swimming along and asked if we could take him on.

"The slightest additional weight meant death for all of us, so we told him that it was no use.

"'All right,' cried the man. 'Good-bye. God bless you all,' and sank."

Just before the "Titanic" went down a collapsible boat was found. It could not be opened properly, but afterwards floated as a raft. Between thirty and thirty-five found a refuge on this. Among them were Mr. Lightoller, the second officer, whose way of escape has already been described; John Thayer, of Philadelphia, Colonel Archibald Gracie, Phillips, the senior Marconi operator, and Bride, his assistant. Most of the men on this raft were ship's firemen, and no attempt was made to keep off other men who swam to it. But of those lost, Colonel Gracie tells a story which will ever redound to the credit of mankind.

"When," he says, "the full complement that the raft would bear had been reached, other men in the water forbore to fight for a place on it, and shouting their blessings and their fare-wells threw up their hands and went down."

Colonel Gracie's own escape from the sinking liner was as marvellous as that of Mr. Lightoller, and the story he tells is wonderful as a great spiritual adventure.

"After sinking with the ship," he said, "it appeared to me as if I was propelled by some great force through the water. This might have been occasioned by explosions under the water, and I remembered fearful stories of people being boiled to death. The second officer has told me that he has had a similar experi-ence.

"Innumerable thoughts of a personal nature having relation to mental telepathy flashed through my brain. I thought of those at home, as if my spirit might go to them to say, 'Good-bye' for ever. . . . Again and again I prayed for deliver-ance, although I felt sure that the end had come.

How the "Titanic" struck the iceberg. The blow was received forward on the starboard side, and tore open the ship's side and bottom from the bows to the engine-room.

"I had the greatest difficulty in holding my breath until I came to the surface. I knew that once I inhaled, the water would suffocate me. When I got under water I struck out with all my strength for the surface.

"I got to air again after a time which seemed to me to be unending. There was nothing in sight save the ocean, dotted with ice and strewn with large masses of wreckage. Dying men and women all about me were groaning and crying piteously.

"The second officer and Mr. J. B. Kayer, jun., who were swimming near me, told me that just before my head appeared above the water one of the 'Titanic's' funnels separated and fell apart near me, scattering the bodies in the water. I saw wreckage everywhere, and all that came within reach I clung to."

Colonel Gracie relates how at last by moving from one piece of wreckage to another he at last reached the raft.

"Soon," he continued, "the raft became so full that it seemed as if she would sink if more came on board her. The crew, for self-preservation, had therefore to refuse to permit any others to climb on board. This was the most pathetic and horrible scene of all. The piteous cries of those around us still ring in my ears, and I will remember them to my dying day.

"'Hold on to what you have, old boy,' we shouted to each man who tried to get on board. 'One more of you would sink us all.' Many of those whom we refused answered as they went to their death: 'Good luck! God bless you!'

"All the time we were buoyed up and sustained by the hope of rescue. We saw light in all directions. Particularly frequent were some green lights, which, as we learned later, were rockets fired in the air by one of the 'Titanic's' boats.

"So we passed the night, with the waves washing over and burying the raft deep in water. We prayed through all the weary night, and there never was a moment when our prayers did not rise above the waves.

"Men who seemed long ago to have forgotten how to address their Creator recalled the prayers of their childhood and murmured them over and over again. Together we said the Lord's Prayer again and again."

Robert Hichens, the quartermaster who had been at the wheel, was, it will be remembered, told off by Mr. Lightoller to look after one of the boats. It had thirty-eight women aboard, one seaman, in addition to the quartermaster himself, and two male passengers, one an Italian boy, and Major Penchen, a Canadian officer.

Hichens took the tiller, and only left it for a few minutes during the night, when a young woman tried to steer, but she was not able to keep the water from coming into the boat, so that Hichens had to take the tiller again.

Upon leaving the ship they rowed away towards a mysterious light, which everyone thought was the light of a French fishing smack. There were other lifeboats in which the crews and passengers believed they saw that phantom ship. It is for this reason that many of the boats were some distance away from the "Titanic." They heard cries and groans, but it was dark. There was no light, and "all we could do," said Hitchens, "was to remain helpless. We only surmised that the cries and groans came from the direction of the sinking ship; they might have come from a capsized boat. Naturally everybody wanted to escape the suction of the sinking ship. It was bitter, freezing weather, and everybody was numbed."

In the boat where Mr. Lowe, one of the ship's officers, had found a place, there were other tragic adventures.

They rescued one man from the sea—an enormous fellow—so heavy, indeed, that every man in the lifeboat was obliged to exert himself to pull the body from the water. This man was bleeding from the nose and mouth, and was evidently rather badly injured. He died soon afterwards.

The survivors were agonised by the terrible shrieks and chorus of groans which, for an hour, arose after the "Titanic" sank.

"We lay just outside the range of the sinking people," said Mr. Lowe, "willing but unable to assist. The sounds we heard rent our hearts, but we were powerless. It would have been impossible for our boat to have rowed into that mass of sinking, struggling folk. It was nothing but a great weltering mass of drowning people, all struggling. Our little boat, if we had rowed into the mass, would have been sunk immediately by the poor strugglers. My boat was nearest to the area of those sinking, and we held ourselves ready to save any poor man who might become detached from the big, confused mass. We were as close as possible, but we could save none."

One of the most tragic things of all in this great tragedy was the number of babies who lost their lives. Their little bodies floated by men who swam until they died. But seven of them had been put into the boats without their mothers. Their names will never be known, perhaps, but they are cared for now, and will never be neglected in life, by people who regard them as the most precious salvage of this great wreck.

The lifeboats were alone now on the sea, and in a little while there were no more swimmers, and no more cries to God. A those. Miss Leader, a lady doctor of New York, tells how this lady behaved with the utmost courage.

"The countess is an expert oarswoman, and thoroughly at home on the water. She practically took command of our boat when it was found that the seamen could not row skilfully. Several women took their place with the countess at the oars, and rowed for a turn, while the weak, unskilled stewards sat quietly in the end of the boat."

Many of the women were only scantily clad. Some of them were without stockings, but the men and women who had come away with warmer clothing shared some of it with those who were suffering intensely from the cold. During the night several people died from exposure. In one of the lifeboats the people were in water up to their knees. Seven of them died and were put overboard. Only those who stood all the time were saved. Among the bodies which floated past the collapsible boat was that of Phillips, the wireless operator. His comrade Bride saw his floating corpse, and grieved for him. Among all those who behaved with unsurpassed courage, Phillips was not least in honour.

Fifteen minutes after the captain had released him from his post of duty he still stayed on, working his "wireless" until the water invaded his cabin. He signalled his last message, and then, with that calm and imperturbable manner which made him scorn to hurry even with death so close to him, he made his way to the deck in time to go down with the "Titanic" when she made her dive into the depths. He swam to the raft, but lay there exhausted until his last

SOME INCIDENTS OF THE DISASTER.

Navy's Memorial Services.

Orders were issued that Divine service on board H.M. ships in Home ports on Sunday, April 21, was also to be a memorial service for those who lost their lives in the foundering of the "Titanic." During the service flags in H.M. ships were half-masted as a mark of respect to the memory of the officers and men of all ranks and ratings of the British mercantile marine and others who were drowned and to their good and seamanlike behaviour after the accident had occurred.

"Birkenhead" Spirit Still Alive.

Before the "Titanic" left Belfast, Captain Smith was asked if old seamen's courage and fearlessness in face of death still existed. He declared if any disaster like that to the "Birkenhead" happened they would go down as those men went down.

Chinese Stowaways Crushed.

Six Chinese, who had hidden beneath the seats of the "Titanic's" lifeboats, are among the survivors. They were not detected until the boats had been taken on board the "Carpathia." Two of their companions, who were also in hiding, were crushed to death by the weight of the other passengers sitting above them.

Famous Jewelled Book Lost.

The copy of Fitzgerald's translation of Omar Khayyam, with Eliku Vedder's beautiful illustrations, famous as "the most remarkable specimen of binding ever produced," went down in the "Titanic." Less than a month ago it realised £405 at auction, where it found an American purchaser. The binding took two years to execute, and the decoration embodied no fewer than 1,500 precious stones, each separately set in gold.

Mr. W. T. Stead's Prophecy.

The curious coincidence is worth recalling that in the Christmas number of the "Review of Reviews" for 1893 a story appeared which bore the title of "From the Old World to the New," by Mr. W. T. Stead. In it he dwelt at some length on the perils of icebergs in the Atlantic.

The scene of the tale was laid on board the White Star liner "Majestic," which was then commanded by the same Captain Smith who went down so gallantly in the "Titanic," and a portrait of Captain Smith was given.

The "Majestic" in the tale drives through fog into floe ice, when suddenly the fog lifts and discloses near at hand a "dazzling array of icebergs, ever shifting and moving. Now and again a great berg would capsize with a reverberant roar." And on one of the bergs a little party of castaways are discovered, who have made their presence known to those on board the ship by telepathy.

There is a tragic note of prophecy in the words of the tale: "The ocean-bed beneath the run of the liners is strewn with the whitening bones of thousands who have taken their passages as we have done, but who never saw their destination."

Millionaire's Last Message.

"If anything happens to me, tell my wife I have done my best in doing my duty," were the last words spoken by Mr. Guggenheim, the New York millionaire, as he stood awaiting his fate on the deck of the sinking "Titanic." The message has been conveyed by a steward to Mrs. Guggenheim.

great silence had settled down upon the sea, and those who had survived were quiet in suffering.

"Abandoned in our little craft," one reads in the narrative of the three Frenchmen, "what fears, what hopes were ours! We were all the time under the illusion that we were seeing lights. We distinguished them on all sides, for how tenaciously does one cling to life! We were perishing with cold. From time to time we shouted to attract the attention of the ships sailing on that sea; but, alas! our voices remained without any echo."

There were brave hearts in those boats who, when they seemed lost for ever in that dark world of loneliness, who had left behind those without whom life will always be desolate, rose above despair and cried "Courage!" to those who were less strong to suffer.

There were women who, when the men were exhausted by fatigue, took the oars and rowed until they, too, were wearied out. There were other women who found themselves in boats with men who had no knowledge of rowing, and whose places they took at the rowlocks. The Countess of Rothes was one of breath failed. Harold Bride, his assistant, has spoken the elegy of that dead comrade:—

"Phillips was a brave man, and I loved him that night when he stuck to his key until the very end. If Phillips had had a chance to go to his room and get warmer clothing, as I did, he probably would be alive to-day. But duty was first with him."

Some of the lifeboats were lashed together so that they should not have drifted wide apart if any steamer came to the rescue. In one of them there was a man with an electric lamp, and in the darkness that little light gave a kind of comfort to those with him as if it were a beacon of hope. Many people tried to forget the horror of their position and to comfort their comrades by praying. In one boat men and women recited the Lord's Prayer over and over again in a kind of chant.

Edward Wheelton, the chief steward of the "Titanic," who had been given a place in one of the lifeboats to look after the women, described his experience during the night.

"At one time, while we were waiting for rescue in the boats, every time we moved our oars they would strike a corpse. Two women died from exposure in our boat while we were floating about waiting for the 'Carpathia.' We buried them over the side of the boat then and there.

"The women in the lifeboats were remarkably calm during the time we were on the water, and the children were very brave. Some women rescued babies which were very small, and a few women voluntarily gave up their lives to protect them.

"Luckily the women in our boat did not see the sinking of the 'Titanic.' It was too dark, and when the day dawned they saw a few sticks and timber floating on the waste of waters, and only then did they realise that something terrible had happened.

"The 'Titanic' was no longer visible above water, and all around us we could see dead bodies floating.

"For the first time the women became terrified, and many wept bitterly, while others seemed dazed."

But at last, as the dawn whitened the sky and light glimmered across the sea, these boatloads of human misery these people of infinite tragedy, saw looming up through the morning haze a ship of good hope. The wireless messages from the "Titanic" had not called in vain. Phillips had not worked and died in vain. Here was rescue close at hand.

A few people had strength and heart to raise a few feeble cheers.

"We shouted 'Hurrah!'" says one of them. "All the boats scattered over the ocean turned their prows towards her. It was a return to life for us."

It was while Atlantic coast residents were thinking about retiring to rest that the wireless station dreaded "S.O.S." signal from the broad Atlantic, at Cape Race, Newfoundland, intercepted the followed by the horrifying news that the "Titanic" had struck an iceberg and was sinking.

The grim message, which was worded "Struck iceberg; badly damaged; help urgently needed," gave the liner's position as latitude 41.46 N., longitude 50.14 W., or, roughly, about 270 miles south-east of Cape Race.

Cape Race sent the message far and wide, and urgent instructions were sent for Government tugs and all shipping in the vicinity to go to the rescue. Relief was felt when the Allan liner "Virginian" flashed back the answer that she also had received the "Titanic's" appeal for help, and was hastening to her assistance. The "Virginian's" wireless operator was able to transmit further messages from the "Titanic," but these brought little comfort, for they stated that the forepart of the vessel was flooded, that she was settling down by the head, and that the passengers were being transferred to the boats.

The "Virginian" was then 170 miles west of the disabled vessel, and when at 12.27 a.m. (Canadian time) she reported that the "Titanic's" signals had ended abruptly the worst was feared. Meanwhile dozens of Marconi operators at sea and along the coast were sending the distress signal over the Atlantic, and from all parts of the apparently deserted ocean highway liners came rushing to the spot indicated.

There were an astonishingly large number of vessels within reach of the "Titanic's" powerful wireless apparatus, and within a very short space of time a dozen liners, representing all nationalities, were heading to the rescue. The "Olympic," sister ship to the disabled leviathan, was one of the first to get the signal, and she was soon racing full speed on a 300-mile course, sending out messages of encouragement as she went.

The "Baltic" was slightly nearer, and flashed back the message that she was 200 miles from the "Titanic" at 3.30 a.m. It is a curious coincidence that the "Baltic" was the first to go to the rescue of the ill-fated liner "Republic," which was wrecked under similar circumstances two years ago, when Jack Binns immortalised the wireless "C.Q.D." signal. This time it was "S.O.S." that the "Baltic" picked up, but officers and crew knew that it meant the same thing, and again she was bound on an errand of mercy.

Other vessels equipped with less powerful transmitters could

Mrs. Smith, the widow of the heroic Captain of the "Titanic," with her infant child.

A few days after the disaster the following pathetic message from Mrs. Smith, widow of the Captain of the "Titanic," was posted outside the White Star offices at Southampton :—

To my fellow sufferers,

My heart overflows with grief for you all, and is laden with the sorrow that you are weighed down with, and which this terrible burden that has been thrust upon us. May God be with us and comfort us all. Yours in deep sympathy,

ELEANOR SMITH.

not announce their intentions to the land stations, but the Allan liner "Parisian," bound for Glasgow, and the Cunarder "Carpathia," bound for Naples, also hurried to the scene of the disaster, while the west-bound Hamburg-America "Cincinnati" and the east-bound "Amerika" and "Prinz Friedrich Wilhelm," the Red Star "Menominee," the French "La Provence" and the German "Prinz Adalbert" all picked up the appeal for help, and turned their heads to latitude 41.46 N., longitude 50.14 W.

It is a remarkable and tragic fact that the Leyland liner "Californian" was less than twenty miles from the "Titanic" when the latter foundered, and if the captain had known of her plight all the passengers might have been saved.

This sensational statement was made by Mr. Lord, the captain of the Leyland liner "Californian," on the arrival of that vessel at Boston on Wednesday, April 24. He denied (says Reuter) that the "Californian" was the steamer passing within five miles which disregarded the distress signals, and added :—

I calculate that we were from seventeen to nineteen miles distant from the "Titanic" on the Sunday evening.

Continued on page 22.
For special sectional drawing and facts about the "Titanic" see next page.

A SECTION DRAWING OF T

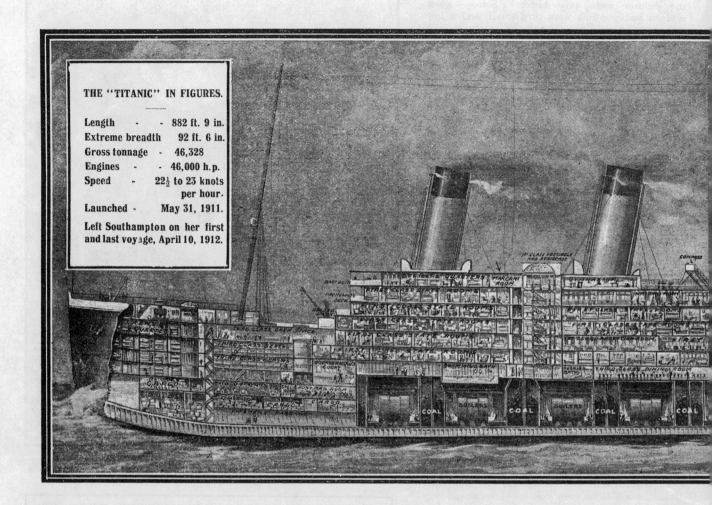

THE "TITANIC" IN FIGURES.

Length	882 ft. 9 in.
Extreme breadth	92 ft. 6 in.
Gross tonnage	46,328
Engines	46,000 h.p.
Speed	22½ to 23 knots per hour.
Launched	May 31, 1911.

Left Southampton on her first and last voyage, April 10, 1912.

THE "TITANIC'S" LARDER.

The "Titanic" took on board at Southampton just before she sailed :

Fresh Meat (lbs.)	... 75,000	Potatoes (tons)	...	40
Poultry (lbs.)	.. 25,000	Ale and Stout (bottles)	...	15,000
Fresh Eggs	... 35,000	Minerals (bottles)	...	12,000
Cereals (lbs.)	... 10,000	Wines (bottles)	...	1,000
Flour (barrels)	... 250	Electroplate (pieces)	...	26,000
Tea (lbs.)	... 1,000	Chinaware (pieces)	...	25,000
Fresh Milk (gals.)	... 1,500	Plates and Dishes (pieces)		21,000
Fresh Cream (qts.)	... 1,200	Glass (pieces)	...	7,000
Sugar (tons)	... 5	Cutlery (pieces)	...	5,000

PREVIOUS GREAT

Following are some of the principal disast

Lives Lo

1911.—September 20 : Olympic (Captain Smith in command) in collision with H.M.S. Cruiser Hawke in Cowes Road ...

1910.—February 9 : French steamer General Chanzy wrecked off Minorca... 20

1909.—January 23 : Italian steamer Florida in collision with the White Star liner Republic, about 170 miles east of New York, during fog. Large number of lives saved by the arrival of the Baltic, which received a distress signal sent up by wireless from the Republic. The Republic sank while being towed to harbour ... ...

1908.—March 23 : Japanese steamer Mutsu Maru sunk in collision near Hakodate 30

1907.—February 21 : G.E.R. steamer Berlin wrecked off Hook of Holland during gale 14

1906.—August 4 : Italian emigrant ship Sirio, bound for South America, struck a rock off Cape Palos 35

1905.—November 19 : L.S.W.R. steamer Hilda struck on a rock near St. Malo and became a total loss 13

1904.—June 15 : General Slocum, American excursion steamer, caught fire at Long Island Sound 1,00

E GIANT LINER "TITANIC."

THE "TITANIC" IN FIGURES.

Lifeboats carried - - 16
Collapsible boats - - 4
Capacity of each lifeboat
50 persons.
Life preservers on board
sufficient for all.
Number of passengers
"Titanic" could carry 3,500
Number carried at time
of disaster - - 1,400
Crew · - - 940

Reproduced by courtesy of "The Illustrated London News."

IPPING DISASTERS.

at sea that have occurred in recent years :

	Lives Lost
1902.—May 6 : Govermorta lost in cyclone, Bay of Bengal ...	739
1901.—April 1 : Aslan, Turkish Transport, wrecked in the Red Sea	180
1899.—March 30 : Stella, wrecked off Casquets	105
1898.—October 14 : Mohegan, Atlantic Transport Co. steamer, wrecked on the Manacles	107
1896.—December 7 : Salier, North German Lloyd steamer, wrecked off Cape Corrubebo, N. Spain	281
June 16 : Drummond Castle, wrecked off Ushant	247
1895.—January 30 : Elbe, North German Lloyd steamer, from Bremen to New York, sunk in collision with the Crathie, of Aberdeen, off Lowestoft	334
1893.—June 22 : H.M.S. Victoria, sunk after collision with H.M.S. Camperdown	359
1878.—March 24 : H.M.S. Eurydice, wrecked off Dunnose Headland, Isle of Wight	300
1852.—February 26 : Troopship Birkenhead struck upon a rock off Simon's Bay, South Africa. The heroism displayed by the men on board has earned them undying renown	454

THE WORLD'S LARGEST SHIPS.

	Gross Tonnage.	Length, feet.	Breadth, feet.	Speed, knots.
*GIGANTIC ...	50,000 ...	1,000 ...	112 ...	—
*AQUITANIA ...	50,000 ...	910 ...	95 ...	23
*IMPERATOR ...	50,000 ...	910 ...	95½ ...	22
TITANIC ...	46,328 ...	883 ...	92·6 ...	22½
OLYMPIC ...	45,324 ...	883 ...	92·6 ...	22½
MAURETANIA ...	31,938 ...	762 ...	88 ...	25
LUSITANIA ...	31,550 ...	762 ...	87 ...	25

* Building or projected.

About 10.30 in the evening we steamed into an immense icefield. I immediately shut down the engines and awaited the daylight, with engines stopped. Our wireless apparatus was not working, so that we did not learn of the "Titanic's" distress until the morning, through the "Virginian," and we then started for the scene of the disaster.

But, as all the world knows, the rescue ship which was first on the scene was the Cunard liner the "Carpathia." After picking up the first call of distress she had rushed at full speed in quest of the sinking ship. Her captain had prayed on the bridge that he might reach the locality given to him in time to take off the passengers. Alas! when he searched the sea he saw nothing of the great vessel, but only those scattered boats filled with dazed and exhausted people.

One of the "Carpathia's" stewards has given a vivid account of how the first boatload of surviving passengers was rescued.

"Just as it was about half day we came upon a boat with eighteen men in it, but no women. It was not more than a third filled. All the men were able to climb up a Jacob's ladder

over the side of the 'Carpathia' was attended by the most heart-rending scenes. The babies were crying, many of the women were hysterical, while the men were stolid and speechless. Some of the women were barefooted and without any headgear."

In a little while after picking up the survivors in the last boat the "Carpathia" swung round and steamed westward on the course for New York.

THE SHIP OF SORROW.

As music and splendour
Survive not the lamp and the lute,
The heart's echoes render
No song when the spirit is mute—
No song but sad dirges
Like the wind through a ruin'd cell,
Or the mournful surges
That ring the seaman's knell.

She was, as all the world has called her, a Ship of Sorrow. On board she had 705 survivors out of those 2,358 souls who had set out from Southampton and Queenstown on the maiden voyage of the world's great ship. She had seventy widows on board weeping for the husbands they would never see again. She had women who were mad with grief and men whose eyes were haunted with horror.

The crew and passengers of the "Carpathia" put all they had at the service of these tragic guests. They gave them their cabins, their clothes, their utmost sympathy and helpfulness. But they could not give them the treasures they had lost, nor take away from them the vision of things seen.

One man among those who were rescued was of valiant service to the ship upon which he had found safety and a new lease of life. It was Harold Bride, the wireless operator. He had had his legs crushed in the collapsible boat by the weight of bodies upon him, and was in great pain.

"I could hardly climb the ladder of the 'Carpathia,' but I was helped up, and the next thing I knew was that I was in a cabin, where a woman rubbed some life into me and gave me some brandy.

"I was taken to the ship's hospital, and afterwards, owing to the pressure of the wireless work, was asked to help the 'Carpathia's' operator. After that I never left the wireless room,

THE SCENE OF THE DISASTER,

The map shows the position of the icebergs on which the "Titanic" struck, with the other liners that hurried to her assistance. She was following the southern or winter track, as shown in the smaller map. The northern track is only followed in summer months, when the ocean is free of ice.

which we threw over the port side. Every one of them was given a glass of brandy or as much coffee as he wanted.

"Between 8.15 and 8.30 we got the last two boats, crowded to the gunwale, almost all the occupants of which were women. After we had got the last load on board the 'Californian' came alongside.

"The captains arranged that we should make straight for New York, while the 'Californian' looked around for more boats. We circled round and round and saw all kinds of wreckage.

"While we were pulling in the boat-loads the women were quiet enough, but when it seemed sure that we should not find any more persons alive then Bedlam came. I hope never to go through it again. The way those women 'took on' for the folk they had lost was awful. We could not do anything to quieten them until they cried themselves out."

John Kuhl, of Nebraska, said it was almost four o'clock in the morning—dawn was just breaking—when the "Carpathia's" passengers were awakened by the excitement caused by coming on a fleet of life-saving boats.

"At that hour," said Mr. Kuhl, "the whole sea was one mass of whitened ice. The work of getting the passengers

but worked night and day sending official and personal messages."

This act of real heroism, the continued devotion to duty by a member of the "Titanic's" crew, even upon the way back, was in keeping with all that story of honour and courage which lifts the tragic drama to great heights of nobility. Into a few brief hours of life, between the darkness and the dawn, when so many souls leapt to eternity, there was time for an epic which will go ringing down the ages with deathless music.

But what of the world beyond this sea of tragedy and glory? What of all those millions who were waiting for news of this maiden voyage of the great "Titanic"?

There also was a tragedy which will not be forgotten in history. When the first whisper of disaster reached America and thence travelled, swiftly as lightning, to Europe, all the civilised world shuddered with a great fear. In England, especially, from which the great ship had gone forth in her pride, there was an anxiety, acute and poignant. Wild rumours were afloat, and seemed to come upon the wind. After the first shock

(Continued on page 24.)

THE "TITANIC'S" LAST PLUNGE.

The following extract from Mr. Beesley's narrative will probably stand as the most vivid and haunting account of the sinking of the "Titanic," as seen from one of the lifeboats :—

"It was one o'clock in the morning. The starlight night was beautiful, but as there was no moon it was not very light. The sea was as calm as a pond.

"In the distance the 'Titanic' looked enormous. Her length and her great bulk were outlined in black against the starry sky. Every porthole and saloon was blazing with light. It was impossible to think that anything could be wrong with such a leviathan were it not for that ominous tilt downward in the bows, where the water was by now up to the lowest row of portholes.

"At about two o'clock we observed her settling very rapidly, with the bows and the bridge completely under water. She slowly tilted straight on end with the stern vertically upwards.

"At the same time the machinery roared down through the vessel with a groaning rattle that could have been heard for miles.

"It was certainly for some minutes that we watched at least 150 feet of the 'Titanic' towering up above the level of the sea, looming black against the sky. Then with a quiet, slanting dive she disappeared beneath the waters. Our eyes had looked for the last time on the gigantic vessel in which we set out from Southampton."

**Lowering away the boat-loads of women and children
from the sinking "Titanic."**

American Continent by wireless, her secret was still shrouded with silence.

On April 18, four days after the foundering of the death-ship, Mr. Franklin made this statement to the Press :—

" The ' Carpathia ' is a ship of sorrow with a company almost mad with grief.

" Definite information concerning the sinking of the vessel is absolutely unavailable. Many messages have been sent to the ' Carpathia,' but we could get no response to our inquiries.

" I have received absolutely no details of the actual loss of the vessel, and we know nothing about what has happened, except such scrappy information as has been contained in the few authentic wireless messages received and already made public.

" Everyone on board the ' Carpathia ' is so overcome that no connected story can be obtained. I have had a code message from Mr. Bruce Ismay, but it relates to business and throws no light whatever on the tragedy."

A horrible fear was created in New York, chiefly owing to the hospital arrangements made by the White Star Company, that serious illness, and possibly mental derangement, existed among the survivors on the " Carpathia."

Besides the arrangements made for ambulances, over forty physicians and nurses were to meet the " Carpathia " at the dock.

The refusal of the " Carpathia " to answer wireless inquiries, even one from President Taft, or to give any information, augmented the fears already expressed and led people to believe that a terrible condition existed aboard.

There were striking scenes at the White Star offices, when hundreds of relatives and friends of the survivors and the lost hurriedly arrived in New York from places all over the country, demanding and pleading for news. Many declared that Mr. Ismay was censoring the wireless facilities on the " Carpathia," and between indignation and tears the poor officials at the offices had an exceedingly hard time.

of ill-news there followed for a time strangely conflicting reports, received from doubtful sources, but reassuring in their character.

" All the passengers have been rescued."

" The ' Titanic ' is being towed to Halifax."

Those assertions of fact cheered men for a little while, buoyed up hearts sick with fear, seemed to give the lie to other reports which alleged that the " Titanic " was sinking.

Crowds besieged the London offices of the White Star line and the London headquarters of the Marconi wireless company. But the officials had no definite news. They could state nothing " officially." They issued reassuring statements. The words of Mr. Franklin, vice-president of the White Star line in New York, were cabled to London. He used the hopeful—and, as it happened, the dreadfully ironic phrase—" The ' Titanic ' is unsinkable."

Then early on the morning of April 14 there came into London newspaper offices one dreadful sentence, from the New York officials, which settled all the rumours in the worst possible way.

" The ' Titanic ' sank at 2.20 a.m."

Even now no details of what had happened came from the mystery and silence of the Atlantic. The number of drowned, the number of survivors, was given from different and still doubtful sources in conflicting reports. Four days later, when the " Carpathia " was in touch with many vessels and with the

Then at last, after all the agony of waiting, the " Carpathia " arrived and gave up her secret. Then from the lips of the survivors the world learnt the story which has now been written—all its horror and all its heroism.

That arrival of the " Carpathia " was the most tragic homecoming of any ship to any port, and there were strange and pathetic scenes on the wharfside.

The rain was pouring down in New York, accompanied by occasional flashes of lightning ; but, in spite of this, hundreds of friends and relatives of the survivors and several thousands of the general public gathered in the neighbourhood of the wharf.

At 8.27 American time (or 1.30 a.m. English time) the " Carpathia " was got into the dock and made fast.

When the " Carpathia " passed the Battery—the extreme point of Manhattan Island, New York City—a crowd of 10,000 people had gathered in the Battery gardens and around the Aquarium. As the vessel passed the point on her way up the Hudson this vast concourse preserved a most impressive—an awe-inspiring silence.

Some well-known passengers who were picked up by the "Carpathia": 1. Lady Duff Gordon (photo by Lallie Charles); 2. Mrs. T. W. Cavendish; 3. The Countess of Rothes (photo by Langfier); 4. Mr. A. H. Barkworth, J.P.; 5. Mrs. J. J. Astor (photo by Underwood); 6. Mr. Bruce Ismay (photo by Ellis & Walery).

The few vessels in the river gave the "Carpathia" a wide berth as she steamed up-stream.

Along 11th Avenue, which runs parallel to the docks, all the way from 12th to 16th Streets—two blocks on either side of the wharf where the liner was docked—a strong police cordon was stretched to prevent the immense crowd getting near the dock.

About a thousand people, nearly all friends and relatives of the survivors, were allowed in the huge shed on the wharf, among them about 500 women dressed in mourning, many of them in tears.

There was also a large detachment of doctors, priests, sisters, and nurses.

The doctors, attendants, and Red Cross nurses, all clad in their white hospital clothing, added a sombre picturesqueness to the scene; several ambulances from St. Vincent and the other big city hospitals were in waiting outside the wharf-shed, the motormen being loaded with clothing and blankets for those in need of them.

It was learned that some of the passengers had died from the effects of cold and exposure.

As soon as the vessel was tied up at her station and the gangway had been run ashore, batches of hospital attendants trooped aboard, carrying a large number of stretchers.

Then as the first survivors came out all the pent-up emotion of that great crowd found expression. A woman shrieked, and it seemed the signal for the great wailing of many women. Men standing silent and bare-headed wept unrestrainedly, and many of those who had been rescued sobbed in mingled joy and grief as they were greeted by their friends and relations. They had come back to life, but—oh God!—the number of those who would never come back!

THE GRIEF OF THE WORLD.

Take them, O great Eternity!
Our little life is but a gust
That bends the branches of Thy tree
And trails its blossoms in the dust.

Swiftly across the world sped the stories of those survivors, and as they were printed swiftly in succeeding editions of the newspapers the world wept also and was stricken with a pity beyond all words. An emotion profound and poignant stirred not only our own nation and kinsfolk, but all civilised peoples. Greater even than the shock which struck the "Titanic" as she went so swiftly through the night to death was the crash to all our human pride, which boasted of conquest over nature, and now was humbled and afraid. Colder even than the icy waters into which those people plunged in the moment of supreme tragedy was the coldness of that terror which struck a mortal chill to the hearts of men when the story of the

"Titanic's" doom was first made known. Sadder than death itself was the pity which went out to those who lived to mourn—to the young widows who were tired of weeping, to the mothers who had lost their sons, to men who had lost their comrades. Not within living memory has any tragedy so stirred the heart and conscience of the world. In Southampton, from which nearly all the crew had gone, there was a piteous lamentation. But all that grief was not sterile. It was expressed in great-hearted charity among all classes, from the richest to the poorest, on behalf of the families left destitute by the loss of their breadwinners. The Lord Mayor of London opened a fund for these sufferers and money poured in unceasingly.

The pity of all people was poured out in another way—in prayer and solemn memorial services for those who were lost. Most solemn and most beautiful was the great memorial service held in St. Paul's Cathedral on Friday, the 19th of April.

Out of the sunlit streets, gay with the beauty of life, there came into the dim twilight, and into the great hush, of St. Paul's Cathedral a vast crowd of men and women, moved by an emotion as poignant as unshed tears.

These people of life came to think of death. They came to express their pity for a great human tragedy, which for a little while, in its awfulness, has made our brotherhood close its ranks like little children who cling together in fear and grief. These people of all classes, of spiritual belief and unbelief, came out of the streets of London to pray for those who have passed through the waters of death, and for those who have been left behind to weep. Seldom has any service in St. Paul's spoken so directly to the hearts of the people who listened, and answered with tears.

Outside, the newspaper placards were telling in grim, black letters, the awful tale of the "Titanic" after the home-coming of the rescue-ship. Out of the long silence there had come the first tidings of how brave men died, and of how love and chivalry shone above the black terror of it all. It was with these messages speaking to them that the great crowds streamed towards the steps of St. Paul's and surged into its nave.

The great doors were closed an hour before the service. The cathedral was full, and many were left outside. It was a vast, black multitude, upon which shafts of light poured down from the high windows. But here and there those glancing rays fell upon coloured ribbons and the flowers in women's hats, even red ties worn by men whose hearts were in mourning. What did it matter how people came dressed?

These people of rank and wealth, these City clerks and shop-keepers, and slum-dwellers had come together into the quiet sanctuary, not in any formal spirit, but in a comradeship of grief, greater than the small conventions of life. Their hearts were unclothed.

A military band picked from the best musicians of the Household troops was grouped below the choir-stalls, and as the hour of the service drew near they played sacred music which came in waves of sound between the pillars and rose in tremulous melody to the high dome. It was music full of sadness, so plaintive sometimes that it seemed like tears of pity falling upon the bowed heads of the people.

After the intoning of the Lesson there was a great silence for a little while. Then suddenly there was a vague, soft noise. It was as though great birds were fluttering their wings outside the windows of the Cathedral. The noise increased. It was the sound of a mighty wind. Louder and louder it grew as the ruffle was played on the massed drums, until the vast Cathedral was filled with a tempest of pro-

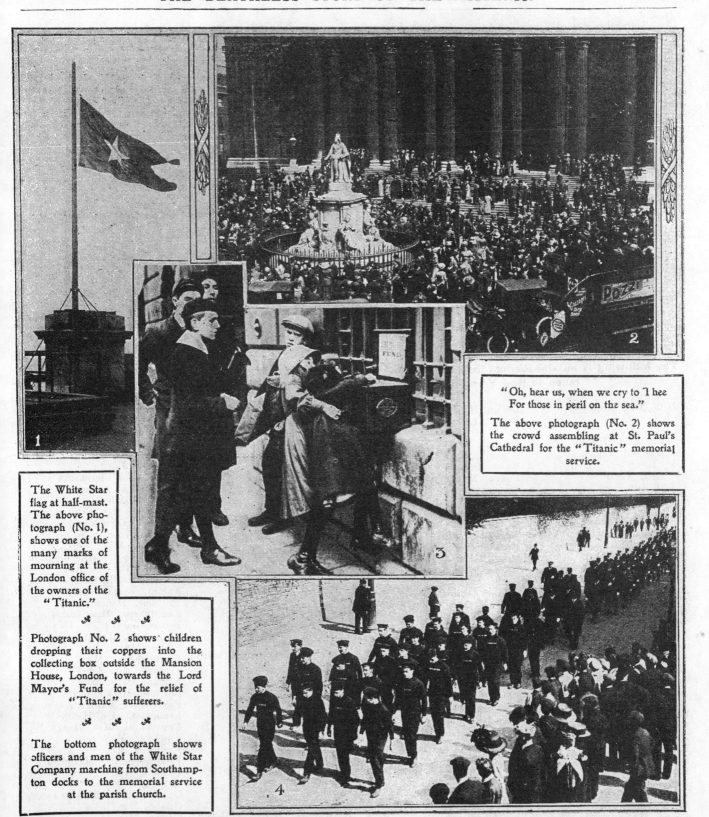

1

The White Star flag at half-mast. The above photograph (No. 1), shows one of the many marks of mourning at the London office of the owners of the "Titanic."

❧ ❧ ❧

Photograph No. 2 shows children dropping their coppers into the collecting box outside the Mansion House, London, towards the Lord Mayor's Fund for the relief of "Titanic" sufferers.

❧ ❧ ❧

The bottom photograph shows officers and men of the White Star Company marching from Southampton docks to the memorial service at the parish church.

"Oh, hear us, when we cry to Thee
For those in peril on the sea."

The above photograph (No. 2) shows the crowd assembling at St. Paul's Cathedral for the "Titanic" memorial service.

digious sound as though all the winds of heaven were rushing over the heads of the people, as though the sea were rising in fury. Then came the boom of great guns, the echo of tremendous thunder, and great crashes as though the sky were rent.

That music of the drums was magnificent and awe-inspiring. It was the story of the "Titanic" in her last agony. Through the dim light between the pillars one saw that mighty ship struck by a mortal blow. One saw her stagger and reel above the waters. One heard the dreadful voice of Nature pronouncing her doom. One heard the groans of her people, the last great noise as she sank into the depths, and then—the gradual stilling of the engulfing waters, and at last—the quietude of death that reigned over the scene of dreadful tragedy.

Now, as when soldiers and heroes go to their graves, the Dead March in "Saul" was played, and again the drums thundered, as though great guns were being fired in the last salute to men who have found victory in death, and there rose that music, sad as death itself, pitiful as the cry of broken hearts, solemn, tragic, yet in the end triumphant as any music that may be heard by the ears of men.

There were many people weeping while that tune of death was played. There were soldiers and sailors in St. Paul's who have heard it played for dead comrades, and they, too, stood erect, with tears streaming down their cheeks, not ashamed of tears. It may be said in all sincerity that the hearts of all these people were stirred to their uttermost depths by thoughts deeper than may be put into words, by a human pity touched by the divine spirit of compassion.

One silent figure seemed to gaze down upon the scene of tragic grief. It was the white statue of Nelson, with his blind eye and sleeveless arm, facing the effigies of other heroes. The spirit of Nelson, who knew the perils of the sea, and who died as bravely as he had lived, must have been present to some of those who knelt below his monument. The watchwords of his life— Courage, Duty, Faith—had not been learnt in vain by those who went down with the "Titanic," upholding the old traditions by their quiet courage in the face of death.

"We humbly leave in Thy Fatherly keeping the souls of Thy servants who have now passed through the waters."

Those words, spoken in a beautiful prayer, were answered by a great Amen. Once again the people rose to sing; this time with a louder and stronger voice, as though strengthened and consoled.

> Eternal Father, strong to save,
> Whose arm hath bound the restless wave,

> Who bidd'st the mighty ocean deep
> Its own appointed limits keep;
> O hear us when we cry to Thee
> For those in peril on the sea.

So the story of the tragedy ends with prayer and tears. It does not end in forgetfulness. As long as the sons of men read the history of heroism so will this story be remembered, with its great warning, its great lesson, its spiritual significance, its deathless drama. Written as it were in letters of gold will be the names of those brave men and women who faced death bravely; who, whatever their condition, died like noble gentlemen and ladies of quality. Many poems have already been written on the sinking of the "Titanic," but the plain story is itself a poem, of the old and high ideals, of the great traditions of human courage and duty; a poem of brave lives snatching victory out of death, and going to their God with a hymn of faith, which will go echoing for ever across the eternal sea.

PASSENGERS WHO WERE SAVED.

The following is an alphabetical list of "Titanic" passengers who were picked up by the "Carpathia"   a taken to New York, as cabled to the White Star Company's London office:

Abbott, Mrs. Rose
Abelseth, Olans
Abelseth, Koran
Abelson, Mrs. Hanna
Abrahamson, August
Ajal, Bemora
Akelseph, Alous
Aks, Filly
Aks, Leah
Allen, Miss Elizabeth Walton
Allison, Master, and Nurse
Aloum, Badmoura
Anderson, Corla
Anderson, Mr. Harry
Andrews, Miss Cornlia I.
Angle, Mrs. Florence
Anton, Louisa
Appleton, Mrs. E. D.
Argenia, Mrs. Genova, and two children
Artonon, V.
Asplund, William
Assim, Marriam
Astlund, Selma
Astlund, Felix
Astor, Mrs. J. J., and Maid
Aubert, Mrs. N., and Maid
Balls, Mrs. Ada A.
Barawich, George
Barawich, Harren
Barawich, Marian
Barkworth, Mr. A. H.
Barlson, Rinat
Bassette, Miss
Batman, Emily
Paxter, Mrs. James
Beane, Mr. Edward
Beane, Mrs. Ethel
Becker, Mrs. A. O., and Three Children
Beckwith, Mr. R. L.
Beckwith, Mrs. R. L.
Beesley, Mr. Laurence
Bentham, Miss Lillian W.
Billa, Maggie
Bing, Lee
Bishop, Mr. D. H.
Bishop, Mrs. D. H.
Blank, Mr. Henry
Bockstrom, Masy
Behr, Mr. K. H.
Boklin, Marie
Boklin, Eugene

Boklin, Helena
Boklin, Latifa
Bolos, Monthora
Bonnell, Miss Caroline
Bonnell, Miss Elizabeth
Boras, John
Bowen, Miss
Bowerman, Miss Elsie
Bradley, Bridget
Bridgett, Ros
Brayton, Mr. George
Brown, Miss E.
Brown, Miss Mildred
Brown, Mrs. J. J.
Brown, Mrs. J. M.
Bryhl, Miss Dagmar
Buckley, Daniel
Bucknell, Mrs. W. and maid
Burns, Miss O. M.
Bury, Mr. Richard
Buss, Miss Kate
Bystrom, Mr. Karolina
Calderhead, Mr. E. P.
Caldwell, Mr. Albert F.
Caldwell, Mrs. Sylvia
Caldwell, Master Alden G.
Cameron, Miss Clear
Cardell, Mrs. Churchill
Cardeza, Mrs. J. W. M.
Cardeza, Mr. T. D. M.
Carr, Ellen
Carter, Mr. Wm. E.
Carter, Mrs. Wm. E.
Carter, Miss Lucile
Carter, Master Wm. C. T.
Casem, Boyan
Cassen, Masef
Cassebeer, Mrs. H. A.
Cavendish, Mrs. T. W. and maid
Chaffee, Mrs. Herbert F.
Chambers, Mr. N. C.
Chambers, Mrs. N. C.
Chandanson, Miss Victorine
Charles, Mr. Wm. E.
Charters, John
Cheang, Foo
Cherry, Miss Gladys
Chevré, Mr. Paul
Chibnall, Mrs. E. M. Bowerman
Chip, Chang

Choonsson, John
Christy, Mrs. Alice
Christy, Miss Juli
Clark, Mrs. Walter M.
Clarke, Mrs. Ada Maria
Cohen, Gust
Collett, Mr. D.
Collett, Mrs. Stuart
Collier, Gosham
Collyer, Mrs. Charlotte
Collyer, Miss Marjorie
Compton, Miss S. R.
Compton, Master A. T.
Connolly, Kate
Coutts, Neville
Coutts, Will
Coutts, Winne
Cornell, Mrs. R. C.
Cribb, L. M.
Crosby, Mrs. Edward G.
Crosby, Miss Harriett
Cummings, Mrs. John Bradley
Dahl, Charles
Daly, Chas.
Daly, Eugene
Daly, Marsella
Daly, P. B.
Daniel, Mr. Robert W.
Daniel, Sara
Darnell, Elizabeth
Davidson, Mary
Davidson, Mrs. Thornton
Davis, Mrs. Agnes
Davis, Master John M.
Davis, Miss Mary
Dean, Ettie, and two children
Deanodelman, Delia
Devany, Margaret
de Villiers, Mrs. B.
Dick, Mr. A. A.
Dick, Mrs. A. A.
Dodge, Mr. Washington
Dodge, Mrs. Washington
Dodge, Master Washington
Doling, Mrs. Ada
Doling, Miss Elsie
Domunder, Theodore
Dorking, Edward
Douglas, Mrs. F. C.
Douglas, Mrs. W. D.
Doyt, Agnes (or Mrs. A. A. Dick)

Drachstedt, Baron von
Draplin, Jennie
Drew, Mrs. Lulu
Drew, Master M.
Driscoll, Miss Bridget
Dugenon, Joseph
Duran, Miss Florentina
Duran, Miss Asimcion
Dyker, Elizabeth
Earnshew, Mrs. Boulton
Eldegrek, Leonek
Eliass, Nicola
Emanuel, Ethel
Emearmaslon, Mr. Renardo
Endres, Miss Caroline
Eustis, Miss E. M.
Falnai, Ermaulman
Fastman, Daniel
Faunthorpe, Mrs. Lizzie
Ferole, Luigi
Flegenhein, Mrs. A.,
Flynn, Mr. J. I.
Fortune, Mrs. Mark
Fortune, Miss Ethel
Fortune, Miss Alice
Fortune, Miss Mabel
Frauenthal, Mr. T. G.
Frauenthal, Dr. Henry W.
Frauenthal, Mrs. Henry W.
Frolicher, Max
Frolicher, Mrs.
Frolicher, Miss Marguerite
Fulwell, Mrs. J.
Gallenagh, Kate
Garside, Miss Ethel
Gibson, Mrs. L.
Gibson, Miss D.
Glynn, Mary
Goldenberg, Mr. Samuel
Goldenberg, Mrs. Samuel
Goldsmith, Emily
Goldsmith, Frank
Gracie, Colonel Archibald
Graham, Mrs. Wm. G.
Graham, Miss Margaret
Greenfield, Mrs. L. D.
Greenfield, Mr. W. B.
Hakaonen, Line
Hamalainer, Mrs. Anna and infant
Hamann, Maria
Hankonen, Elina
Hanson, Jenny

Hanson, Miss Jeannie
Harder, Mr. George A.
Harder, Mrs. George A.
Harper, Mr. Henry Sleeper and Manservant
Harper, Mrs. Henry Sleeper
Harper, Miss Nina
Harris, Mr. George
Harris, Mrs. Henry B.
Hart, Mrs. Esther
Hart, Miss Eva
Haven, Mr. H.
Hawksford, Mr. W. J.
Hays, Mrs. Charles M.

Hokkronen, Ellen
Hold, Mrs. Annie
Holverson, Mrs. A. O.
Hosono, Mr. Masabumi
Howard, Mary
Hoyt, Mr. Frederick M.
Hoyt, Mrs. Frederick M.
Hyman, Abraham
Ilett, Miss Bertha
Ismay, Mr.
Jacobson, Mrs. Amy F.
Jacques, Mrs.
Jansen, Carl
Jap, Jules

Jousef, Hannah
Jousef, Mariam
Jousef, Thamine
Jusefa, Carl
Jusefa, Manera
Karlson, Einar
Keane, Miss Nora A.
Kelly, Annie
Kelly, Mary
Kelly, Mrs. F.
Kennedy, John
Kenton, Miriam
Kenyon, Mrs. F. R.
Kesorny, Florence

Laroche, Miss Louise
Leach, Miss Jessie
Leader, Mrs. F. A.
Lehman, Miss Bertha
Lesneur, Mrs. Gustav
Lines, Mrs. Ernest H.
Lines, Miss Mary C.
Lindstroem, Mrs. J.
Lindquist, Eihar
Longley, Miss Gretchen F.
Louch, Mrs. Alice
Ludgais, Amo
Lulu, Nella
Lundegreen, Aurora

BOAT DRILL ON A WHITE STAR LINER.

The first photograph shows a boat being lowered away, with the officers and crew in cork jackets. The second photograph gives a general view of the boat deck, with the boats at the davits ready for lowering. The bottom photograph is that of the crew at quarters swinging out a lifeboat.

Hays, Miss Margaret
Hedman, Oscar
Hemvig, Croft
Herman, Mrs. Jane
Herman, Miss Kate
Herman, Miss Alice
Herronen, Hilda
Hewlett, Mrs. Mary D.
Hillsfrom, Hilda
Hip, Ching
Hippach, Mrs. Ida S.
Hippach, Miss Jean
Hocking, Mrs. Elizabeth
Hocking, Miss Nellie
Hoffman, Mr. Lolo
Hoffman, Mr. Lones
Hogeboom, Mrs. John C.

Joblom, S.
Jenson, Carl
Jermyn, Miss Mary
Jermyn, Annie
Jerserac, Inav
Johannson, Oscar
Johanson, Verendt
Johnnanson, Alice
Johnnanson, Elenora
Johnnanson, Oscar L.
Johnsen, Harold
Johnsila, Eric
Josburg, Siline
Joseph, Katherine
Joseph, Mary
Joseph, Nigel
Jousef, George

Kimball, Mr. E. N.
Kimball, Mrs. E. N.
Kink, Louisa
Kinorn, Krikoraen
Kockovean, Erickau
Kolsbottel, Anna
Koucher, Miss Emile
Krigesne, Jos
Kuram, Anna
Kuram, Frans
Lam, Hah (Ali)
Lamore, Mrs. Amelia
Lang, Fang
Lang, Hee
Lare, Eleoneh
Laroche, Mrs.
Laroche, Miss Simonne

Lunden, Olga
Lundstrom, Imrie
Madigan, Maggie
Madill, Mrs. Georgette Alexandra
Maioni, Miss Ruberta
Mallet, Mrs.
Mallet, Master A.
Mallie, Bertha
Maloney, Mrs. R.
Manga, Margaret
Manga, Mr. Paula
Manv, Juvio
Maran, Bertha
Massey, Marion
Marechal, Pierre
Marlkarl, Hauwakan

Marrigan, Margaret
Marrion (Mannion), Margaret
Marshall, Mr.
Marshall, Mrs.
Marshall, Miss Katey
Marson, Adele
Marvin, Mrs. D. W.
Mathesen, Frithiof
Mathgo, Karl
Mauman, Hanne
Meyer, Mrs. Edgar G.
McCarthy, Katie
McCoy, Bernard
McCoy, Agnes
McCoy, Alice
McCoy, Ernest
McDearmont, Miss Leila
McDermott, Delia
McCormick, Thomas
McGovan, Mary
McGovan, Anna
McGowan, Miss A.
McGough, Mr. J. R.
McKaren, John
Mellers, Mr. William
Mellinger, Mrs. Elizabeth, and Child
Merigan (Harrigan)
Messelmolk, Anna
Messelmolk, G. D.
Messewacker, Guilliam
Messewacker, Arcina
Midtago, Carl
Minahan, Mrs. W. E.
Minahan, Miss Daisy
Missulmona, Amina
Mock, Mrs. Philippe
Mocklaire, Ellen
Modelmot, Celia
Montharck, Annie
Montharck, Gurio
Montharck, Halim
Moran, Bertha
Moore, Belle
Moore, Neciman
Morgan, Mr.
Morgan, Mrs., and Maid (Miss Francatelli)
Moss, Albert
Moubarck, Burns
Muhun, Erikorian
Mullen, Kate
Mulder, Theodore
Mulvehill, Bertha
Murphy, Kate
Murphy, Maggie J.
Murphy, Nora
Naseraill, Miss Adelia
Neckard, Said
Neket, Marin

Nelso, Helmina J.
Nelson, Bertha
Nelson, Carlo
Nern, Hannah
Newell, Miss Alice
Newell, Miss Madeline
Nevatey, Margaret
Newsom, Miss Helen
Nicolo, Jancoli
Nicolo, Elias
Niskenen, John
Nouberek, Halin
Noubarek, Jiron
Nubulaket, Samula
Nye, Mrs. Elizabeth
Nyhan, Anna
Nysten, Anna
Oamb, Nicola
O'Brien, Hanna
O'Dwyer, Nelly
O'Keefe, Patrick
O'Leary, Nora
Olivia, Miss
Ollmson, Sourly
Olman, Virma
Olsen, Arthur
Ongalen, Helena
Ornout, Mr. Alfred F.
Osman, Mara
Osplund, C. Anderson
Oumson, ——
Oxenham, Mr. Thomas
Padro, Mr. Julian
Pallas, Mr. Emilo
Parrish, Mrs. L. Davis
Parsons, Ernest
Patos, Coterina
Patro, Hobesa
Penasco, Mrs. Victor
Pears, Mrs. Thos.
Person, Eames
Pericault, Miss A.
Peuchen, Major Arthur
Phillips, Miss Alice
Picard, Benoit
Pinksy, Miss Rosa
Portaluppi, Mr. Emilio
Potter, Mrs. Thomas, jun.
Quick, Mrs. Jane
Quick, Miss Phyllis
Quick, Miss Vera W.
Ranelt, Miss Appic
Reardon, Hannah
Reibon, Anna
Renago, Mrs. Naman J.
Renouf, Mrs. Lillie
Rheims, Mr. George
Richards, Mrs. Emily
Richards, Master William
Richards, Master George
Ridsdale, Miss Lucy
Robert, Mrs. Edward S.

Rogers, Miss Selina
Rolmane, Mr. C.
Rosenbaum, Miss
Roth, Sarah
Rothes, the Countess of, and Maid (Miss Mayoni)
Rothschild, Mrs. M.
Rugg, Miss Emily
Ryan, Edward
Ryerson, Mrs. Arthur
Ryerson, Miss
Ryerson, Miss Susan
Ryerson, Master
Saalfield, Mr. Adolph
Saleman, Mr. A. L.
Salkjelsock, Anna
Sandstrom, Agnes
Sandstrom, Beatrice
Sandstrom, Margaret
Sap, Jules
Schabert, Mrs. Paul
Schurbint, John
Schurlinch, Jane
Scunda, Assed
Scunda, Famine
Segisser, Miss Emma
Serepeca, Miss Augusta
Seward, Mr. Frederick K
Shelley, Miss Imanita
Shine, Axel
Shine, Ellen
Shutes, Miss E. W.
Sibelrome, Agnes
Sibelrome, Rose
Silven, Miss Lyyli
Silverthorne, Mr.
Silvey, Mrs. Wm. B.
Simmonius, Mr. Oberst Alfons
Simpson, Miss Anna
Sincock, Miss Maud
Sindo, Beatrice
Sinkkonen, Miss Anna
Sjablom, Annie
Slayter, Miss H. M.
Sloper, Mr. Wm. T.
Smith, Miss Marion
Smythe, Salia
Snyder, Mr. John
Snyder, Mrs. John
Sofia, Anna
Spedden, Mr. Frederick O.
Spedden, Mrs. Frederick O.
Spedden, Master R. Douglas
Spencer, Mrs. W. A., and Maid
Stahelin, Dr. Max
Stanley, Amy
Steffanson, Mr. H. B.
Stengel, Mr. C. E. H.
Stengel, Mrs. C. E. H.
Stephenson, Mrs. W. B.

Stone, Mrs. George M., and Maid
Strander, Julo
Strauss, Maid of Mrs.
Strinder, Juho
Smith, Mrs. L. P.
Submaket, Fituasa
Sulici, Nicola
Sunderland, Victor
Sundman, Julian
Svenson, Severin
Swift, Mrs. Frederick Joel
Taussig, Mrs. Emil
Taussig, Miss Ruth
Taylor, Mr. E. Z.
Taylor, Mrs.
Thayer, Mrs. J. B. and Maid
Thayer, Mr. J. B., jun.
Thorneycroft, Florence
Tonglin, Gunner
Toomey, Miss Ellen
Trant, Mrs. Jessie
Trenobisky, Berk
Troutt, Miss E.
Tucker, Mr. G. M., jun.
Turgen, Anna
Tukula, Hedvig
Turnguist, H.
Vagil, Adele J.
Walcroft, Miss Nellie
Ware, Mrs. Florence
Warren, Mrs. F. M.
Waters, Miss Nellie
Watt, Mrs. Bessie
Watt, Miss Bertha
Webber, Miss Susie
Weisz, Mrs. Matilda
Wells, Miss Addie
Wells, Miss J.
Wells, Master Ralph
West, Mrs. Ada
West, Miss Barbara
West, Miss Constance
White, Mrs. J. Stuart and Maid
Wick, Miss Mary
Wilhems, Mr. Chas.
Wilkes, Ellen
Widener, Mrs. George D. and Maid
Willard, Miss Constance
Williams, Mr. C.
Williams, Mr. R. M., jun.
Wilson, Miss Helen
Wimhormstrom, Amy E.
Woolner, Mr. Hugh
Wright, Miss Marion
Yazlick, Salamy
Young, Miss Marie
Zenn, Phillip
Zuni, Fabin

₊ *This list, issued by the White Star Company on April 20, shows many discrepancies with the Board of Trade's official figures.*

Officers and Members of Crew who were saved:

C. H. Lightoller (2nd officer)
H. Pitman (3rd officer)
J. Boxthall (4th officer)
G. Lowe (5th officer)
J. Haines (boatswain's mate)
H. Bailey (master-at-arms)

Stewardesses, etc.

Miss S. Strap
Mrs. K. Gold
Mrs. E. Leather
Mrs. A. Martin
Miss M. Sloan
Miss V. Jessop
Miss M. Gregson
Miss Smith
Mrs. K. Bennett
Mrs. McLaren

Miss E. Marsden
Mrs. A. Pritchard
Mrs. Roberts
Mrs. N. Robinson
Miss B. Lavington
Mrs. E. Bliss
Mrs. M. Slocombe
Miss A. Caton.

———

J. Foley (storekeeper)
S. Hennings (lamps)
W. Wimie, A.B.
J. Perks
R. Bright
G. Rome
J. Poing Derstoc
G. McGough

W. Meiles
W. Peters
P. Hogg
T. Jones
E. Archer
F. Flett
G. Symons
A. Jewell
F. Church
R. Hitchens
Cavell
Priest
Blake
W. White
Lindsey
Pearce
Noss

Hunt
Godley
Thrasher
Beacha
Combes
Clark
Mansea
Pinsted
Pelboun
Casper
Nutlearn
Podesta
F. Oliver
C. Hascoe
Avery (fireman)
Doel (fireman)
F. A. R. Mason

Strict
Dore
Sparkman
Fryer
Crummins
Kerrish
Oliver
Dymond

J. Piggott
L. Moore
F. Orman
J. Bewley
P. McCarthy
F. O. Evans
V. Hopkins
J. Forward

F. Louis
H. A. Etches
A. Tessinger
H. Crawford
C. Cullen
A. Cunningham
J. Johnstone
W. Ward

S. H. Nichols
H. Phillamore
F. Tirrel
J. G. Willgery
J. Whitter
J. Hart
A. Pearcey
H. J. Prior
L. Hyland
F. Port
W. S. Halford
A. E. R. Lewis
P. J. Savage
C. Foley
A. Pugh
J. Maynard
J. Ellis
A. Windbank
A. Simmons
Barrett
Hendricksen
Puen (?)
Threllfall
Collins
Moore

Anxious crowds at London and Southampton: 1. Reading the lists of survivors
outside the White Star Offices in London;
2. Awaiting news inside the office; 3,
Relatives of the crew studying the lists at
Southampton.

Triggs
Cooper
Harty
Harris
Rue
Dilley
Draper
Knowles
Panger
A. White
Scott
Judd
Thompson
Self
Hogan
W. Wright (plate washer)
G. Whiteman (barber)
W. Fitzpatrick (steward)
Miss R. Bowker (restaurant)
Miss M. Martin (restaurant)
Paul Mange (kitchen clerk)
F. Marten
H. Rose
J. Colgan
R. Hardrick
J. Joughin (chief baker)
H. Neal (baker)
C. Burgess (baker)
C. Mills (butcher)
P. Bull

Perry
Sheath
J. Taylor
W. H. Taylor
Shears
Fredericks
S. Humphreys
J. Lee
J. Horsewell

S. Evans
W. Brice
W. Lucas
J. Anderson
J. Scarrott
W. Horder
A. McMicken
E. Brown
F. Ray

E. J. Gay
R. P. Fropper
W. E. Eyerson
J. W. Gibbons
W. J. Williams
W. Seward
J. Chapman
C. Andrews
A. Burrage

Officers and Crew of the "Titanic."

The following is a complete official list of the officers and crew who sailed on the "Titanic." Unless otherwise stated, they resided at Southampton:—

Edward J. Smith, Winn Road, Southampton, captain.

H. F. Wilde, Grey Road, Walton, Liverpool, chief mate.

W. M. Murdoch, Belmont Road, first mate.

C. H. Lughloller, Netley Abbey, second mate.

H. J. Pitman, Castle Cary, Somerset, third mate.

J. S. Poxhall, Westbourne Avenue, Hull, fourth mate.

H. J. Lowe, fifth mate.

James Pelloody, St. James' House, Grimsby, sixth mate.

William F. N. O'Loughton, Polygan House, Southampton, surgeon.

J. Edward Simpson, Pakenham Road, Belfast, surgeon.

J. Bell, Canute Road, chief engineer.

W. Farquharson, Wilton Avenue, senior second engineer.

J. H. Hesketh, Garrett Avenue, Liverpool, junior second engineer.

N. Harrison, Coventry Road, junior second engineer.

G. F. Hosking, Avenue Road, Itchen, senior third engineer.

E. C. Dodd, Queen's Parade, junior third engineer.

L. Hodgkinson, Arthur Road, senior fourth engineer.

J. N. Smith, Millars Road, Itchen, junior fourth engineer.

B. Wilson, Richmond Road, Shirley, senior assistant engineer.

H. G. Harvey, Obelisk Road, Woolston, junior assistant second engineer.

J. Shepherd, Bellevue Terrace, junior assistant second engineer.

C. Hodge, Ivy Road, Woolston, senior assistant third engineer.

F. E. G. Coy, Portswood Road.

James Fraser, Tennyson Road, junior assistant third engineer.

H. R. Dyer, Middle Street, senior assistant fourth engineer.

A. Haveling, South Front, junior assistant fourth engineer.

A. Ward, Manor House, Romsey, junior assistant fourth engineer.

Thomas Kemp, Cedar Road, assistant fourth engineer.

F. A. Parsons, Bugle Street, senior fifth engineer.

W. D. Mackie, Margery Park Road, Forest Gate, E., junior fifth engineer.

R. Millar, North Street, Alloa, fifth engineer.

W. Moyes, Douglas Terrace, Stirling, senior sixth engineer.

W. M. E. Reynolds, Lagon Villas, Belfast, junior sixth engineer.

H. Creese, Enfield Grove, Woolston, deck engineer.

T. Millar, Meadow Street, Belfast, assistant deck engineer.

G. Chiswall, High Street, Itchen, boilermaker.

H. Fitzpatrick, Nelson Street, Belfast, junior boilermaker.

Peter Sloan, Clovelly Road, chief electrician.

A. S. Alsopp, Malmesbury Road, second electrician.

H. June, Bullar Road, assistant electrician.

Alfred Middleton, Sligo, assistant electrician.

A. W. May, York Street, Northampton.

J. Hutchinson, Onslow Road, joiner and carpenter.

A. Nicholls, St. Cloud, Oak Tree Road, 'bosun.

J. Maxwell, Leighton Road, carpenter.

A. Haines, Grove Street, boatswain's mate.

T. King, Middlemarket Road, master-at-arms.

H. Bailey, Oswood Road, master-at-arms.

J. Foley, Queen's Road, storekeeper.

S. Hemming, Kingsley Road, lamp trimmer.

C. Proctor, Southview Road, chef.

A. Bocketay, Oakbank Road, assistant chef.

H. Stubbings, Onslow Road, cook.

H. Maynard, Earls Road, cook.

H. W. McElroy, Polygon House, purser.

R. L. Barker, Mayhaith, Old Shirley, purser.

C. Holcroft, Canterbury Road, Seacombe, clerk.

E. W. King, Currin Rectory, Clones, clerk.

F. R. Rice, Kimberley Drive, Crosby, clerk.

G. F. Turner, Hedley Gardens, Chiswick, stenographer.

F. G. Phillips, Farncombe, Godalming, telegraphist.

H. St. Bride, Bannister's Hotel, telegraphist.

L. Gatti, Harbour Road, Southampton, manager of restaurant.

Francisco Nanni, Aubert Road, Finsbury Park, N., head waiter.

Giuseppi Bochet, London, second head waiter.

R. Boroker, Little Sutton, Cheshire, first cashier.

M. E. Martin, Apsley Villa, Acton, second cashier.

W. A. Jeffrey, Apsley Villa, Acton, controller.

H. Vine, Apsley Villa, Acton, assistant controller.

Albert Ervine, Maryfield, Belfast, assistant electrician.

William Kelly, Claude Road, Dublin, writer.

William Duffy, Garton Road, Itchen, writer.

A. Rous, Ratcliffe Road, writer.

R. J. Sawyer, Bevois Street, window cleaner.

W. Hardie, Winton Street, window cleaner.

Mess Stewards.

W. A. Makeson, Western Esplanade.
John Coleman, Mortimer Road, Itchen.
S. Blake, Holyrood House.
George Gumery, Canute Road.
C. W. N. Fitzpatrick, Millbrook Road.

Quartermasters.

S. Humphreys, Duke's Road.
W. Wynn, Church Street.
A. Olliver, Anderson's Road.
R. Hickens, St. James's Street, Dongola.
G. Rowe, Henry Street.
A. Bright, Firgrove Road.
W. Perkis, Victoria Road, Bitterne.

Look-Out Men.

S. Symons, Fanshaw Street.
F. Fleet, Norman Road.
J. A. Hoff, High Street.
F. Evans, Deal Street.
A. Jewell, College Street.
R. R. Lee, Threefield Lane.

Able Seamen.

W. Weller, Holyrood House, Southampton.
W. Lucas, Corporation Flats.
F. Bradley, Threefield Lane.
G. Moore, Graham Road.
W. H. Lyons, Orchard Lane.
J. Forward, Sailors' Home.
A. Horswick, Derby Road.
E. Archer, Pitswood Road.
F. Osman, High Street.
Stephen J. Davis, Duncan Street, Landport.
C. Taylor, High Street.
F. Crouch, Port Isaac, Cornwall.
B. Terrell, Trinity House Street.
W. McCarthy, Gratton Hill Road, Cork.
T. Jones, Nesbitt Street, Liverpool.
E. Buley, Cliff Road, Woolston.
C. H. Pascoe, High Street.
H. Holman, Britannia Road.
D. Matheson, Everton Street.
G. Clench, Chantry Road.
G. Church, Chantry Road.
F. Tamlin, Southampton Street.
Robert Hopkins, Woodstock Road.
W. C. Peters, Ludlow Road.
J. Anderson, Couzens Court.
W. Smith, Bridge Road.
F. O. Evans, Bond Street.
J. McGough, St. George Street.
J. Scarrott, Albert Road.
P. Vigett, Windsor Terrace.
W. Brice, Lower Canal Walk.
J. Poingdestre, Elan Road.

Storekeepers.

A. Kenzler, Bleckendon Terrace.
A. Foster, Norwich Front.
H. Rudd, Chapel Street.
C. Newman, Latimer Street.
Edward Parsons, Robert's Road, Southampton.
H. H. Thompson, Eastwood, Lumsden Avenue, Southampton.
J. W. Keran, Avenue Road.
F. W. Prentice, Denzil Avenue.
G. Ricks, Hanley Road.
Arthur J. Williams, Peter Road, Walton.
C. F. Morgan, Bessboro' Road, Birkenhead.
E. J. W. Rogers, Oxford Avenue.
S. A. Stap, Bidston Avenue.

Firemen.

W. Small, Liverpool, Russell Street.
James Keegan, Liverpool, West Place.
T. Threlfall, Liverpool, St. Martins Court.
F. Walker, Hants, Avenue Road.
Thomas Ford, Liverpool, Russell Street.
C. Hendrickson, Northumberland Road.
W. Mayo, Castle Street.
T. Davies, Church Lane.
J. Norris, Spa Road.
T. Graham, Downpatrick Street.
E. Wateridge, Millbrook Street.
J. Wyett, Millbank Street.
J. Thomas, Newman Street.
C. Otken, Northumberland Road.
John Jactopin, Dukes Road.
C. Altrams, Charles Street.
C. Painter, Mortimer Road.
H. Sparkman, Spring Road, Sholing.
F. Reeves, Cable Street.
W. Lindsay, Coleman Street.
W. Jarvis, Canal Walk.
R. Price, Houndwell Gardens.
W. Brugge, Sailors' Home, Southampton.
T. Knowles, Lymington.
W. Butt, Cawle Road.
G. Rickman, Derby Road.
H. Smither, Ash Tree Road.
E. McGaw, Broadlands Road.

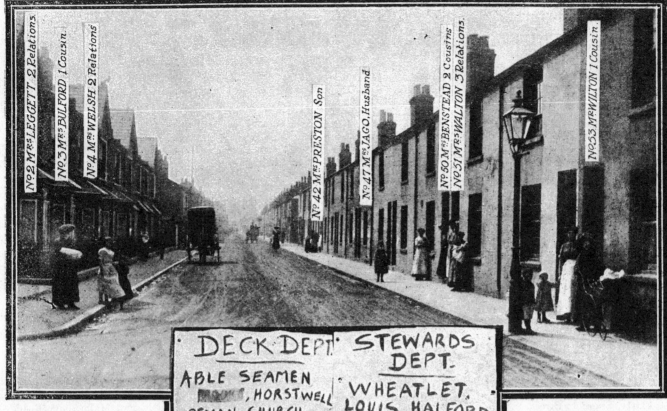

In the top photograph the marked houses read:

No 2 Mrs LEGGETT 2 Relations.
No 3 Mrs BULFORD 1 Cousin.
No 4 Mrs WELSH 2 Relations.
No 42 Mrs PRESTON Son.
No 47 Mrs JAGO, Husband.
No 50 Mrs BENSTEAD 2 Cousins.
No 51 Mrs WALTON 3 Relations.
No 53 Mr WILTON 1 Cousin.

The notice board reads:

DECK DEPT   STEWARDS DEPT.
ABLE SEAMEN   WHEATLET.
FROST, HORSTWELL   LOUIS HALFORD,
OFMAN, CHURCH   SAVAGE, ROSS,
McCARTHY, BEWLAY, & SMUK.
HASCOE, HOPKINS,
McGOUGH, POINGDERSTR   SHOULD BE
& MELLES
                   T. WHITELEY
SHOULD BE
                   F. TOMS   Saloon Stud
HORSWELL
F. OSMAN   W.S. HALFIRD   "   "
F. CLINCH   3rd CL Stud
W. McCARTHY   C.G. SAVAGE
E.J. BULEY
C.H. PASCOE   H. ROSS   "   "
R.J. HOPKINS   Cook
McGOFF   K. SMITH
POINGESTER   Stewardess
S. WELLER

NOTE,
LYONS

J. Haggan, Sailors' Home, Southampton.
G. Combes, Coleman Street.
W. Light, Grove Street.
A. Mayzes, Commercial Street.
M. Pusey, School Lane, Hythe.
R. Triggs, Canal Walk.
R. Cooper, Dukes Road.
F. Young, Russell Street.
J. Dilley, Threefold Lane.
E. Gradidge, Redcliffe Road.
A. Blatherstone, Mount Street.
A. Tizard, Lord York Street.
A. Shiers, Peel Street.
E. Hannan, Oxford Terrace.
E. Harris, Belgrave Road.
George Nettleton, Empress Road.
F. Mardle, Back of Walls.
H. Siniar, South Road, Clapham.
W. Watson, York Street.
F. M. McAndrews, New Capley Bridge.
S. Graves, North Front.
R. Hopgood, Ramsay Road.
D. Hanbrook, York Street.
J. Padesta, Chantry Road.
W. Neithear, High Street.
N. Toas, Bond Street, Southampton.
Thomas James, College Street.
J. Blaney, Sailors' Home, Southampton.
J. Taylor, Manor Road.
A. Head, Russell Street.
W. Sims, Charlotte Street.
J. J. Moore, Arthur Road.
J. Barnes, Woodley Road, Woolston.
J. Diaper, Derby Road.
T. Bradley, Green's Court.
E. Tegs, Kempley Road.
J. Ward, Hames Street.

F. Barrett, King Street,
J. Mason, Wycombe Court, French Street.
F. Pugh, Peel Street, Northam.
T. Blake, Peel Street, Northam.
W. Ferris, Hanover Buildings.
H. Cooper, St. George's Street.
W. Cherrett, Nelson Road.
E. Williams, Canal Walk.
J. McGregor, Briton Street.
G. W. Baily, Brook Street, Woolston.
J. Fraser, Sailors' Home, Southampton.
J. Chorley, Regent Street.
T. Hart, College Street.
T. Hunt, Queen Street.
F. W. Barrett, Bevors Street.
A. Slade, Chantry Road.
W. Ball, Brintons Road.
Thomas Slade, Chantry Road.
T. Laley, Spulling Road, East Dulwich.
G. Kemish, Shirley Road.
A. Streets, Lion Street, Shirley.
G. Roberts, Withers Street.
B. Moss, St. Peters Road.
G. Slade, Chantry Road.
George Milford, Graham Street.
E. Blien, Pound Street.
T. Instance, Guillaum Terrace.
W. Saunders, Edward Street.
C. Rice, Oriental Terrace.
R. Turley, Sailors' Home, Southampton.
W. McCastlan, French Street.
A. Black, Briton Street.
C. Biddlescomb, Kentish Road.

Southampton, where the majority of the crew lived, was a city of sorrow as soon as news of the disaster became known. The top photograph shows Milbank Street, one of Southampton's Streets of Mourning, with several of the bereaved homes marked. The other photograph is that of one of the notice boards outside the White Star Company's local office, where the names of rescued members of the crew were posted. Mistakes in cabling names were corrected from time to time, and each correction lifted a burden of sorrow from some home.

B. Hands, St. Michael's House.
M. W Golder, Lansdowne Road.
William McQuillan, Sea View Street, Belfast.
John Noon, Sailors' Home.
B. Cunningham, Briton Street
C. J. Hewert, Larndorf Road.
W. Burrows, Elm Street.
Thomas Shea, Briton Street.
J. Hall, Westgate Street.
C. Barlow, St. Mary's Road.
G. Beauchamp, Redbridge Road.
F. Saunders, Sussex Terrace.
Thomas McAndrill, Sailors' Home.
J. Cummins, King Street.
G. Marget, Elm Street.
S. Sullivan, Marsh Lane.
E. Biggs, College Street.
Archibald Scott, Lower Ditches.
J. Shaw, Northumberland Road.
Frank Holden, Albany Road
W. McRae, Three-fold Lane.
R. Adams, Pound Terrace Road.
D. Cacceran, Sailors' Home.
F. Harris, Belle View Road, Gosport.
A. May, York Street.
F. Shafper, Brunswick Square.
W. Mintram, Chapel Road.
G. Hallett, Church Road.
H. Oliver, Nichols Road.
G. Snellgrove, Cecil Avenue.
C. Sangster, Bevon Street.
Charles Barnes, York Road.
Frank Painter, Bridge Road.
C. Judd, Derby Road.
J. Brown, Russell Street.
E. Flarty, Stamford Street.
F. Rendell, Woodley Road.
G. Thresher, Mount Pleasant Road.
J. Taylor, Russell Street.
W. Bessant, Henry Road.
W. Major, Oriental Terrace.
G. Burnett, Deal Street.
E. McGurney, College Street.
F. Wardner, Endle Street.
W. Hurst, Chapel Road.
Thos. Kerr, Hartley Street.
F. Mason, Waverley Road.
A. Burroughs. Adelaide Road.
A. Witcher, Nelson Place.
G. Godley, Mount Street.
T. Morgan, Sailors' Home, Southampton.
W. Vear, Spa Gardens.
H. Vear, Spa Gardens.
H. Allen, French Street.
W. Cross, Ludlow Road.
F. Drel, Richmond Street.
J. Pearse, Drummond Street.
John Coffy, Sperbourne Terrace.
E. Burton, Chapel Street.
W. H. Taylor, Broad Street.
H. Noss, Back Lane.
S. Doyle, Orchard Place.
E. Denville, Orchard Lane.
W. Clet, Paget Street.
W. Hodges, Britannia Road.
J. Priest, Lower Canal Walk.
H. Blackman, College Street.
L. Dymond, Farmers Court.
G. Pond, Sailors' Home, Southampton.
C. Light, Back of Walls.
Wm. Murdock, Sailors' Home, Southampton.
J. Thompson, Howe Street, Liverpool.
J. Canner, Shamrock Road, Woolston.
A. Curtis, Kingsley Road.
S. Collins, Sailors' Home, Southampton.
F. Taylor, Queen's Street.
H. Stubbs, Spa Gardens.
J. Richards, Summers Street.

Trimmers.

J. Dawson, Briton Street.
W. McIntyre, Floating Bridge Road.
W. Hinton, Cumberland Street.
James McCann, St. George's Place.
T. Casey, Sailors' Home, Southampton.
W. Evans, Manor Road, Hitchin.

J. Haslin, Sailors' Home, Southampton.
F. Carter, Cross Street.
W. Saunders, Suffolk Square.
A. Foyle, Charlotte Place.
F. White, Northbrook Road.
R. Proudfoot, Pear Tree Green.
S. Maskell, Albert Road.
B Brewer, Foundry Lane.
B. Gosling, Lower York Street.
J. Read, Nelson's Place.
J. Brooks, Lion Street.
William Wilson, Queen's Street.
H. Lee, Bevors Street.
A. Farrang, St. Mary's Place.
G. Cavell, South East Road, Tholing.
R. Morrell, Malmesbury Road.
J. Bevis, Empress Road.
A. Morgan, Threefield Lane.
H. Brewer, Palmerston Road.
R. Reid, Wickham's Court.
H. Coe, Cross Court.
H. Perry, Rye Terrace.
Thomas P. Dillon, Sailors' Home.
A. Dore, Mount Street.
E. Smith, St. Mary's Buildings.
E. Tegs, Kempley Road.
A. Hunt, French Street.
F. Harris, Willow Street.
J. Bellows, Bell Street.
W. Morris, Marine Parade.
S. Webb, Sailors' Home, Southampton.
W. Snooks, Sailors' Home, Southampton.
A Hebb, Bell's Court.
R Moore, Manor Cottage, Headbourne Street.
B. Mitchell, Bevois Valley.
C. Shillaher, Nelson Road.
H. Stocker, Middle Road, Sholing.
A. J. Fagle, Lym Street. Southampton.
F. Watts, St. Michael's Home, Southampton.
H. Ford, Royal Oak.
W. Skeater, King Street.
F. Sheath, Bell Street.
A. Penney, Chantry Road.
H. Calderwood, Sailors' Home, Southampton.
W. Binstead, Endle Street.
G. Kearl, Bay Road, Sholing.
H. Wood, St. Michael's Home, Southampton.
J. Hill, Kingsland Square.
C. Blake, Rumbridge Street, Totton.
F. Long, Sidford Street.
E. Perry, Ryde Terrace, Southampton.
P. Blake, Floating Bridge Road.
T. White, Colbert Street, Northam.
H. Crabb, Furgrove Road.
W. Long, Maine Terrace.
S. Gosling. French Street.
E. Snow, Lower Canal Walk.
T. Preston, Millbank Street.
G. Pelham, Sailors' Home, Southampton.
G. Green, Howards Grove.
E. Ingram, Lower York Street.
J. Avery, Hills Road.
J. Cooper, Pound Street.
G. Allen, Short Street.
W. Fredericks, Elm Road, Chapel.
R. Carr, Malvern Cottages, Winchester Road.
E. Elliott, Sailors' Home, Southampton.

Greasers.

A. White, Southampton Place.
J. Jukes, Moor Green. West End.
Fred Kanchensen, Latimer Street.
C. Keare, Chantry Road.
G. Phillips, Grove Street.
F. Beattie, Sailors' Home, Southampton.
A. Self. Romsey Road.
T. Palles, Upper Palmer Street.
O. Fastman, Cecil Avenue.
A. Veal, Imperial Avenue.
G Prangnell, Brew House Court.
T. Rungem, Middle Road.
W. Pitfield, Albert Road.
C. Olive, College Street.

F. Godwin, Totton.
F. Woodford, Clovelly Road.
M. Stafford, Southhook Square.
A. Morris, Short Street.
W. Bott, Nichols Road.
J. Couch, Canton Street.
T. McInerney, Colston Street.
J. Kirkham, Chapel Street.
T. Fay, Stamford Street.
J. Jago, Millbank Street.
J. Tozer, Challis Street.
R. Baines, Union Place.
R. Moores, Northumberland Road.
D. Gregory, Floating Bridge Road.
E. Castleman, North Road, St. Deny's.
F. Scott, Clifford Street.
F. Goree, Belvedere Terrace.
J. Kelly, Woodleigh Road.
J. Dannon, St. George's Street.

Stewards.

A. Latimer, Glenwylin Row, Waterloo (chief).
George Dodd, Morris Road (second).
J. S. Wheat, Cobden Gardens (assistant second).
W. T. Hughes, Ivybank, Dyer Road (assistant second).
William Moss, Charlton Road (saloon).
W. Burke, Bridge Road (second saloon).
A. J. Goshawk, Coventry Road (third saloon).
W. Osborne, Hewitts Road.
John Strugness, The Poligon.
A. Dubb, Atherley Road.
W. Rovell, Liverpool, Malmesbury Road.
J. Smillin, Glasgow, Malmesbury Road.
James Johnston, Hants, Seamens' Home.
A. A. Howe, Cliff Road, Itchen.
C. D. Mackay, Hilton Road.
Henry Ketchley, Northcote Road.
W. Dyer, Stafford Road.
W. Brown, Ormskirk, Hillsidie Avenue.
C. Whalton, Liverpool, Bilmoor Road.
E. Brown, Holyhead, Suffolk Road
A. Kutchling, Derby Road.
B. Oaket, Vaudrey Street.
A. Best, Malmesbury Road.
W. House, Derby Road.
H. Cove, London, Shirley Park Road.
W. Lucas, London, Cardigan Terrace.
Tom Weatherstone, Kenilworth Road.
E. Spinner, Oxford Street.
A. W. Barringer, Padswell Road.
A. McMickca, Suffolk Road.
F. D. Ray, Avenue Road, Palmer Park.
H. I. Lloyd, Oxford Street.
J. Shea, Portsmouth Road.
F. Allsop, Obelisk Road.
J. H. Boyes, Clovelly Road.
G. Knight, Ludlow Road.
A. J. Littlejohn, Weston Terrace, Chapel Road.
Ernest T. Barker, Grand Parade, Harringay.
R. Jones, Portland Terrace.
H. Bristow, Shortlands, Kent.
B. Boughton, Richmond Street.
P. Keen, Rugby Road.
F. Crafter, Albert Road.
J. McMullin, St. Mary's Road.
H Fairall, Surrey Street, Ryde.
William Lake, Florence Hotel.
S. Nicholls, Brunswick Square.
F. Toms, Hillside Square.
E. Thomas, Avenue Road.
J. E. Cartwright, Western Terrace.
R. G. Smith, Stafford Road.
M. Rowe, Bridge Road.
George Evans, Richmond Road.
T. Turner, Terminus Terrace.
G. Cook, Bridge Road.
A. Coleman, Oaktree Road.
J. Symons, Church Street.
J. Ranson, Knowle, Bristol.
W. Cherubin, Mile Street, Newport, I.W.
H. Crisp, Macnaughten Road.

Wm. Burrows, Hanover Street, London.
J. H. Stagg, Commercial Road.
J. L. Pury, Manor Road, Itchen.
L. White, Romsey Road.
S. Rummer, Cranbury Road.
A. Stroud, Shirley Road.
L. Hoare, High Street.
A. Lawrence, Oxford Street.
E. Hendy, Paynes Road.
A. Derrett, Hillside Avenue.
A. M. Bagot, Park Road, Freemantle, Southampton.
C. Casswill, Oxford Avenue.
W. Pryce, Heatherdene, Newlands Road.
W. Ward, Millbrook Road.
B. Fish, Blackbury Terrace.
L. Whiteley, St. John's Park, Highgate.
E. Burr, Above Barr.
T. Veal, Forster Road.
F. Wormald, Pestwood Road.
P. Deslands, Portswood Road.

J. Boyd, Cranbury Avenue.
J. Butterworth, Priory Road.
J W. Robinson, Vine Cottage, Carlisle Road.
J. R. Diverage, Cowle Road.
F. C. Simmons, Middlebrook Road.
Joseph Dolley, Devonshire Road.
Thomas Holland, Walton Village.
T. W. H. Cowles, Camden Place.
Ernest E. T. Freeman, Hanley Road.
W. Boston, Hanley Road.
W. Hawksworth, Lemon Road.
P. W. Fletcher, Liscombe Avenue.
E. Abbott, North Road.
R. E. Burke, Southampton Road, Chandlerford.
C. Back, Weymouth Terrace.
Brooke Webb, Hanley Road.
E. Hamilton, Shirley Road.
J. Stewart, Earles Road.
A. T. Broome, White Lodge.

W. Gwann, Shirley Road.
A. Hayter, Mayflower Road.
T. Clark, Hillside Avenue.
R. Wareham, Park Road.
R. Allen, Kenilworth Road.
F. McCarthy, Charlton Road.
W. Anderson, Queen's Terrace.
G. R. Davis, Hillside Avenue.
R. Ide, Lyon Street.
R. C. Geare, Grove Road.
H Wittman, Richmond Road.
S. Gill, Suffolk Avenue.
J. Hill, Cromwell Road.
E. Harris, Greenhill Road, Winchester.
C. Edwards, Brunswick Square.
J. W. Marriott, Chilworth Road
J. Akerman, Rochester Road.
S. Stebbings, Richfield Road.
H. Fellowes, Bridge Road.
C. Jackson, Graham Road.
W. Henry, Romsey Road.

THE TERRORS OF THE NORTH ATLANTIC.

Our photograph shows a typical iceberg in the North Atlantic. A drawing on an earlier page gives a striking idea of the vast bulk of ice concealed beneath the water.

James Toshuch, Malmesbury Road.
W. Taylor, Morris Road.
W. F. Kingscote, Elgin Road, Freemantle, Southampton.
T. Warwick, Totton.
A. E. Lane, Victoria Road.
A. C. Thomas, Brunswick Place.
R. Butt, Carole Road.
J. McGrady, Platform Tavern.
P. Ahler, Northumberland Road.
P. Kilford, New Road.
H. Bruton, St. Andrew's Road.
F. Hartnell, Harcourt Road.
W. W. Dawes, Nelson Road.
C. Lydiatt, Brunswick Square.
A. Mellor, Carlton Place.
E. Bagley, Woodside Road.
George Lefevre, Orchard Place.
D. E. Saunders, Albert Road.
A. D. Harrison, Oakley Road.
H. Yearsley, Gloucester Passage.
G. F. Crowe, Milton Road.

T. Wright, Stern Street, Shepherd's Bush.
E. Bessant, Shirley Park Road.
J. Painton, Shakespeare Avenue.
Ernest R. Olive, Hanley Road.
S. Holloway, Hartington Road.
W. Carney, Caird Street, West Derby Road, Liverpool.
Alfred King, Dyer Road.
T. Allen, Short Street.
L. Perkins, Emsworth Road.
W. A. Watson, Oakley Road.
C. H. Harries, Short Street.
A. Barrett, North Road.
A. Mishelany, Criterion Restaurant.
E. T. Corben, Floating Bridge Road.
Samuel Ryler, Athenlay Road.
F. Morris, Shirley Road.
H. Broome, Thetis Road.
E. Major, Criterion Restaurant.
F. Pennol, Imperial Avenue.
Thomas Baxter, Atherley Road.
John P. Penrose, Southern Road.

E. J. Guy, College Terrace.
J. Scott, Upper Canal Walk.
S. Hiscock, Chantry Road.
F. Hopkins, Fanshaw Street.
W. Bunnell, Kingsfold Road.
E. Hogue, Alison Grove, Dulwich Common.
C. Light, Thorney Hill, near Christchurch.
J. A. Bradshaw, Portland Street.
P. Ball, Windsor Terrace.
Donald Campbell (clerk).
W. F. Janaway, St. George Road.
A. Cunningham, Charlton Road.
T. Hewitt, Devonfield Road, Aintree.
A. Cranford, Cranbury Avenue.
P. P. Ward, Ridgefield Road, Shirley.
W. Bishop, High Street.
E. Ward, Richmond Terrace.
T. Donoghue, Ludlow Road.
Charles Culling, Warburton Road.
William Faulkener, Romsey Road.

Thomas O'Connor, Linaker Lane.
W. McMurray, Empress Road.
C. Stagg, Pulver Street, Liverpool.
H. Roberts, Mildmay Road, Bootle.
Charles Crimplin, Shakespeare Avenue.
S C. Siebert, Harold Road, Shirley.
A. Thussinger, French Street.
W. Bond, Handley Road.
E. Stone, St. Andrew's Road.
H. Etches, Gordon Avenue.
G. Brewster, Carlton Place.
J. Walpole, Stafford Road.
B. Tucker, Suffolk Avenue.
G. Levett, Chilworth Road.
F. Smith, Ordnance Road.
F. B. Wrayson, Southampton Street.
J. Monks, Livingstone Road.
John Hardy, Oakleigh, Highfield (chief second-class).
H. Jenner, Bellevue Road.
R. Sconnell, Foundry Lane, Freemantle.
P. W. Conway, Bentham Road, S. Hackney.
M. Rogers, Greenhill Avenue, Winchester.
R. J. Davies, The Polygon.
H. Philleine, Priory Road.
G. Bailey, Brooklands, Shepperton.
Alan Franklin, Egremont, Newton Road.
R. Parsons, Polygon Road.
R. Russell, Anchor Hotel, Redbridge.
G. E. Moor, St. Mary's Road.
W. Ridout, Queen Anne Buildings.
F. H. Randall, Empress Road.
A. Whitford, Richmond Street.
A. Jones, Woodfield Charlton Road.
W. G. Dashwood, Sailors' Home.
M. V. Meddleton, Felsham Road, Putney.
T. Seaton, Middle Road, Sholing.
N. Daughty, Bridge Road.
C. Harris, Short Street.
F. Benham, Bridge Road.
E. Stroud, Malmesbury Road.
C. Jensem, Morris Road.
W. E. Ryerson, Salop Road, Walthamstow.
R. Pfraffen, Washington Terrace.
John Charman, Latimer Street.
Joseph Heinen, Malden Hill House, Lewisham.
C. W. Samuel, Osborne Road.
Peter Alinger, Marsh Lane.
J. Hawkesworth, Milton Road.
Jacob V. Gibbons, Harbour View, Studland Bay.
F. Terrell, Grove Street.
W. Williams, Northumberland Road.
H. Christmas, Bruitons Road.
B. Lacey, Southampton Road, Salisbury.
W. Penny, Lodge Road, Southampton.
J. T. Wood, Morford Road, Upper Clapton.
C. Andrews, Millbrook Road.
G. Robertson, Mount Street.
H. Humphreys, Rockstone Lane.
G. H. Dean, King Edward Avenue, Shirley.
R. Owen, Earls Road.
H Gunn, Bridge Road.
W. T. Kerley, Woodminton Cottages, Salisbury.
W. H. Nichols, Kent Road.
R. J. Pacey, Cambridge Villa, Millbrook Road.
F. Kelland, Commercial Street, Bitterne (library steward).
F. W. Edge Clovelly Road.
J. Witter, Dorchester Road, Woolston.
H. Bulley, Carrabrooke, Britannia Road.
J. Chapman, Belherne Road.
W. Perren, Bellemore Road.
G. Hinckley, Oxford Street.
J. G. Widgery, Oxford Street.
G. Barrow, Carminster, Foundry Lane.
F. Ford, Oxford Street.
C. Smith, Hollydean, Portsmouth Road.
W. Boothby, Ivey Road, St. Denys.
G. Mackie, Winchester Road.

J. Byrne, Balfour Road, Ilford.
C. Reed, Derby Road.
G. Beeden, Shrewsbury Road, Harlesden.
E. W. Hamblyn, Norman Villas, Dyer Road.
H. Bogi, Crescent, Eastleigh.
E. H. Petty, Orchard Place.
E. F. Stone, Shirley Road.
W. Suvary, Shirley Road.
C. Cook, Chantry Road.
A. Harding, Station Cottages, Swaythling.
J. Longmuir, The Crescent, Eastleigh.
Arthur E. Jones, Ludlow Road.
R. Fisher, Duncan Street, Portsmouth.
F. Hambley, Clarendon Road.
A. Burray, Emsworth Road.
Mrs. Snape, Well Lane, Sandown.
Mrs. Wallis, St. Mary's Place.
James Kiernan, Inglewood, Billemoor Road.
S. F. Geddunary, Emsworth Road.
L. Mullar, Oxford Street (inspector and steward).
A. Pearcey, Kent Road.
W. Dunford, Bridge Street.
J. Brookman, Richmond Street.
H. P. Hill, Oxford Street.
F. Ford, Burtons Road.
C. Taylor, Oxford Street.
R. Bristow, Western Road.
F. Edbroke, Lake Road, Portsmouth.
J. Mabey, Grove Road.
A. D. Nichols, Dulford Avenue.
G. Chitty, Bevons Valley Road.
V. Rice, Thackeray Road
S. G. Barton, College Street.
W. D. Cox, Thirley Road.
A. Ackerman, Rochester Street.
J. A. Prideaux, Cotlands Road.
H. J. Flight, Bellevue Street.
S. Daniels, Albert Road.
R. Mankle, Brintons Road.
E. B. Ede, Manor Farm Road.
W. Sivier, Westbourne Grove Mews, Paddington.
L. Knight, Spring Lane, Bishopsgate.
A. Mantz, Grove Street.
H. Ingrouville, Hoxbury Bridge Road.
J. Hart, Foundry Lane.
G. Talbot, Lemon Road.
W. E. Foley, Monsons Road, Chapel.
T. Port, Rockthorne, Foundry Lane.
H. Finch, French Street.
M. Thaler, Station Road, W. Croydon.
W. H. Egg, Brixton Trent Road.
E. Hilemot, Orchard Place.
M. Leonard, Chatwell Street, Belfast.
Richard Halford, Latimer Street.
H. R. Baxter, Shirley Road.
A. E. Peasel, Richmond Street.
T. Mullin, Onslow Road.
C. J. Savage, Harold Road.
G. Evans, Nightingale Grove.
H. Prior, Padwell Road.
A. Pugh, Orchard Lane.
C. Cecil, Millbrook Road.
H. Ashe, Wiresdale Road.
C. Crispin, Station Hill, Eastleigh.
J. White, Thackeray Road.
W. Wright, Easworth Road.
W Willis, Derby Road.
A. Lewis, Ratcliffe Road.
T. Ryard, Albert Road.
W. T. Fox, Totton.

Stewardesses.

M. Slocombe, Leopold Terrace, Tottenham.
A. Caton, Highbury Hill, London.
K. Gold, Glenthorne, Bassett.
Annie Martin, Posbrock Road, Portsmouth.
E. L. Leather, Park Road, Port Sunlight.
M. Bennett, Cranbury Avenue.
M. Gregson, Lawland Road
B. C. Jessop, Shirley Road, Bedford Park.
M. Sloan, Kersland Crescent, Belfast.

E. Marsden, West Marland Street.
T. E. Smith, Balmoral, Cobbett Road.
M. K. Roberts, Chestnut Grove, Nottingham.
H. McLaren, Shirley Road.
A. Pritchard, Rosslyn Road, East Ham.
A. Robinson, Shirley Road.
B. Lavington, Manor Farm, Headbourne Road, Winchester.
E. Bliss, Upper Park Road, New South gate.
K. Walsh, Church Road.

Cooks.

W. Summons, Thackeray Road.
F. Gallop, Briton Street.
C. Ruskimmel, Park View.
M. J. Mew, Hillside, Bitleme Park.
W. Slight, Hillside, Bitleme Park.
J. Lovell, Highlands Road.
W. Caunt, Sidney Road.
J. Hutchinson, Oxford Street.
J. R. Ellis, Dukes Road.
G. Ayling, Wilton Street.
J. Orr, Coleman Street.
H. E. Beverley, Brunswick Square.
H. Welch, Northaven, Bond Road, Swatling.
P. Dawkins, Fleming Road.
F. J. Beauman, Londesborough Road Southsea.
C. Coombs, Dykes Road.
Wm. Thorley, John Street.
H. Jones, Regent Street.
W. Bedford, Manor Road, Itchen.

Scullions.

F. A. J. Hall, Sidney Road.
W. Bull, Chandos Street.
J. Collins, Ballicar Road, Belfast.
H. Ross, Inkerman Road, Woolwich.
F. Martin, High Street, Fareham.
Joseph Colgan, West Street.
W. Platt, Belgrave Road.
G. Allen, Grove Street.
G. King, Thrafield Street.
W Inge, Stratton Road.
Reginald Hardwicke, Heysham Road.
Wm. Beere, Avenue Cottages, Shirley.
C. Smith, Grove Street.
Harry Shaw, Towcester Street, Liverpool.
A. Simmons, Bevon Valley Road.

Bakers.

C. Joujhi, Elmhurst, Leighton Road, (chief).
J. Giles, Lime Street.
J. J. Davies, Earlfield Road.
W. Hine, Lyndhurst.
C. Burgess, Bridge Road.
H. Neal, Cliff Road.
J. Smith, Torpio Road.
L. Wake, Gloucester Passage.
G Ching, Bevons Valley.
F. Barnes, Parsonage Road.
A Barker, Kingsworthy, Winchester.
E. Farenden, South Street, Emsworth.
A Lauder, Fanshaw Street.
G. Feltham, St. Denis Road.

Butchers.

A. Mayhew, Stafford Road (chief).
T. Topp, Millbrook Road, Farnborough.
F. Roberts, Derby Road.
C Mills, Albert Road.
T. Parker, Upper Boyle Street.
W. Wilsher, Britannia Road.
H. G. Hensford, Malmesbury Road.

Attendants, Barbers, Waiters, Ship's Cooks, etc.

J. B. Crosbie, St. Dunstan's Road.
W. Ennis, Bedford Road, Southport.
Leonard Taylor, Sherbourne Road, Blackpool.
A. H. Whiteman, Ivy Bank, Dyer Road.
A. White, Parnell Road, Portsmouth.
H. Keene, Oakley Road.
P. Gill, Waverley Road.

H. Johnston, Albert Road.
H. Hatch, Portswood Road.
Ernest Brice, Apsley Villa, Acton.
Charles Furvey, Apsley Villa, Acton.
J. Phillips, Jessie Terrace, Southampton.
E. Yorrish, care of Gatti.
C. Scavino, Gatti.
Angelo Knotto, Gatti.
P. Pourpe, Gatti.
R. Urbini, Gatti.

David Beux, Gatti.
B. Bernardo, Gatti.
Louis Biatti, Gatti.
J. Monros, Gatti.
Alfonso Meratti, Gatti.
G. Lavaggi, Gatti.
Lornetti Mario, Gatti.
Rinaldo Ricadone, Gatti.
Abele Rigozzia, Gatti.
Giovanni de Martiro, Gatti.

Jean Vicat, Gatti
Other Men Engaged by Messrs. Gatti Were:
Henry Jaillet.
Georges Jouanwault.
Pierre Vilvarlarge.
Morel Conraire.
Louis Dornier.
Jean Pachera.
Giovanni Monteverdi.
Louis Desornini.

REQUIEM MASS FOR THE "TITANIC" DEAD.

A remarkable photograph of the impressive service at Westminster Cathedral, at which
many distinguished Roman Catholics were present.

Ettera Vahassori, Gatti.
Narsisso Bazzi, Gatti.
Enrics Ratti, Gatti.
Guitio Casali, Gatti.
Geno Jesia, Gatti.
Giovanni Batihoe, Gatti.
Robert Nieni, Gatti.
V. Gilandino, Gatti.
Benj. Theyn, Aubert Park, Finsbury.
E. Poggi, Bowling Green House.
E. Dinapoly, Gatti.
Orovello Louis, Gatti.
Alonzia B. Aptix Di Antonio, Gatti.

Maurice de Treacq, Gatti.
Albert Provatin, Gatti.
Sebastino Serantino, Gatti.
Itilo Donnati, Whitefield Street, Tottenham Court Road.
Aber Pedrini, Bowling Green House, Southampton.
P. Rousseau, Gatti
G. Biatrix, Gatti.
Henri Bollin, Gatti.
Auguste Contin, Gatti.
Claude Janin, Gatti.
Adrian Charboisson, Gatti.

Adolph Maltman.
H. Voegelin.
Gerald Groxlaude.
Jean Blumet.
George Aspilagt.
C. Tietz.
Carlo Leiz.
F. Bertoldo.
Paul Mange.
G. Salussolia.
E. Testoni.
Tazez Sartori.

LORD CHARLES BERESFORD'S TRIBUTE TO THE "BLACK SQUAD."

A fine tribute to the engineers and boiler room staff of the "Titanic," the "black squad," who stood to their posts in the bowels of the ship, to the last, was paid by Lord Charles Beresford in a letter to the "Times." He wrote :—

"In the late appalling disaster to the 'Titanic,' perhaps the greatest in maritime history, attention has rightly been called to the bravery, resolution, and chivalrous gallantry of Captain Smith, the officers, seamen, band, and passengers, who were true to the spirit of manly duty of the English-speaking races in a sudden and terrible emergency.

"Many comments have been justly made regarding the heroism on deck, but nothing has been said of the heroism below.

"I respectfully submit that unintentionally the dauntless heroism of those employed in the engine and boiler room (such as the carpenter and his crew), have been passed over without comment.

"Nothing can exceed the heroism of the captain, officers, and seamen of the ship; but officers and seamen are the first to offer a whole-hearted tribute of unbounded admiration to those working below, as they well know how often the real grit and courage of the officers and men of these departments is called upon in moments of emergency.

"It is stated that the lights were burning until a few minutes before the ship took her final plunge.

"This proves that the officers and men below remained at their posts when they must have known that death—the most terrible and painful that it is possible to conceive—awaited them at any minute, either by the bursting of a steampipe or water rising in a compartment.

"It is certain that those working below must have known the awful danger the ship was in long before anybody else, but they remained at their posts, resolving to die sooner than come on deck and create a panic or attempt to save themselves.

"Those below must have heard the muffled sound of the ice tearing through the ship's side.

"Within ten minutes or a little more they knew that the pumps would not check the rising water, yet for over two hours they remained at their posts, as was evinced by the lights burning and the few of them who were saved being picked up after the ship went down.

"That so many people were saved was due to the fact that those working below remained at their posts working the dynamos and kept the lights burning, and never came on deck to state what had really happened.

"Again and again the indomitable pluck and discipline of those who work below in the engine and boiler rooms is illustrated when some terrible disaster of the sea occurs, but on no occasion have these traits been more brilliantly shown.

"It should be remembered that those below work in confined spaces, watertight doors closed, often in intolerable heat, with a roar of machinery making orders difficult to understand.

"A man will face death with greater equanimity on deck than working below under the incidents I have mentioned.

"Working below really requires more fortitude and pluck.

"All honour and respect to those men whose names will be recorded on the roll of fame for gallantry in a sudden and unlooked-for disaster. But I am sure the survivors of this shocking catastrophe will agree with me in placing those who worked below on 'The right of the line.'"

At the time of the disaster, says "The Times," the first watch in the engine-room was on duty, the second watch was off duty, and the third watch was asleep. When the alarm was sent round every man on board ship, from captain to boy, would be called to take up his allotted station. The engine-room staff ordinarily take part in boat drill. The fact that none of the engineers was saved is attributed to the circumstance that they would all be required at their stations below, not only in the engine-rooms and stokeholds, but looking to the auxiliary machinery, the watertight bulkheads, and other matters which are under control of the chief engineer. Until released from duty, which could only be at the last moment, it is unlikely that any one of them would be able to go up to the higher decks. This would not apply, at all events in the same degree, to the case of the stokers, and those stokers who were off duty below would, no doubt, take their part with the seamen in getting away the boats. These men, therefore, would have an opportunity to attempt to save themselves when the ship made her final plunge. The names of at least two stokers appear in the list of the saved.

One who has served as a chief engineer of an ocean liner and has had experience in some of the largest steamships said that the tribute paid by Lord Charles Beresford to the engineers of the "Titanic" in his letter was fully deserved. The work of the engineering staff in the modern vessel was essentially of a character involving great personal risk at all times and a minimum of personal recognition.

"None would ever know," he added—"for not a soul emerged from the engine room—what happened during the last hours of the vessel's existence. From his experience of other, and happily less serious, accidents, he conjectured that, in accordance with practice, when the collision occurred every one of the engineers off duty hurried to the engine room and there, down in the bowels of the ship, remained until the awful moment when the hulk rose for its final plunge into the depths. From the outset the engineers could have been under no misconceptions as to the extent of the damage to the vessel, though probably they were, for the most part, firmly of opinion that the vessel was practically unsinkable. They kept the lights in operation, and, equally important, kept up the power for the wireless system. Water was probably pouring in beyond all possibility of their doing any good with the pumps, and the boiler rooms were doubtless first flooded. The magnitude of the disaster must have been early evident to the engineers, and escape would not have been impossible, but that would have meant shirking their duty. Only those who had served in the engine room could form any idea of the terrible incidents which probably preceded the final disappearance of the vessel. The devotion of her engineering staff was beyond praise."

STATEMENT BY COMMITTEE OF SURVIVORS.

When the "Carpathia" arrived at New York, the following statement, drawn up by a committee of the surviving passengers of the "Titanic" was handed to the Press :—

"We the undersigned surviving passengers of the 'Titanic,' in order to forestall any sensational and exaggerated statements, deem it our duty to give to the Press a statement of the facts which have come to our knowledge, and which we believe to be true.

"On Sunday, April 14, 1912, at about 11.40 on a cold, star-lit night, the ship struck an iceberg, which had been reported to the bridge by the look-out, but not early enough to avoid collision. Steps were taken to ascertain the damage and save the passengers and the ship. Orders were given to put on lifebelts, the boats were lowered, and the usual distress signals were sent out by wireless telegraphy, and rockets were fired at intervals.

"Fortunately, a wireless message was received by the 'Carpathia' about midnight. She arrived on the scene of the disaster about 4 a.m. on Monday. The officers and crew of the 'Carpathia' had been preparing all night for the rescue work, and for the comfort of the survivors. These were received on board with the most touching care and kindness, every attention being given to all, irrespective of class. Passengers, officers, and crew gladly gave up their state rooms, clothing, and comforts for our benefit; all honour to them.

"The English Board of Trade pas-

sengers' certificate on board the 'Titanic' allowed for a total of approximately 3,500. The same certificate called for lifeboat accommodation for approximately 950, in the following boats :—Fourteen large lifeboats, two smaller boats, and four collapsible boats. Life preservers were accessible in apparently sufficient number for all on board. The approximate number of passengers carried at the time of the collision was :—

First class	...	...	330
Second class	...	...	320
Third class	...	...	750
Total	...	...	1,400
Officers and crew	...	940
Total	...	...	2,340

Of the foregoing about the following number were rescued by the "Carpathia" :—

First class	...	...	210
Second class	...	...	125
Third class	...	...	200
Officers	...	...	4
Seamen	...	...	39
Stewards	...	...	95
Firemen	...	...	71
Total of crew	...	...	210
A total of about	...	775

"The number saved was about 80 per cent. of the maximum capacity of the lifeboats. We feel it our duty to call the attention of the public to what we consider the inadequate supply of life-saving appliances provided for modern passenger steamships, and recommend that imme-

diate steps be taken to compel passenger steamers to carry sufficient boats to accommodate the maximum number of people carried on board.

"The following facts were observed, and should be considered in this connection :

"In addition to the insufficiency of lifeboats, rafts, etc., there was a lack of trained seamen to man the same (stokers, stewards, etc., are not efficient boat handlers). There were not enough officers to carry out the emergency orders on the bridge and to superintend the launching and control of the lifeboats, and there was an absence of searchlights. The Board of Trade rules allow for entirely too many people in each boat to permit the same to be properly handled.

"On the 'Titanic' the boat-deck was about 75 ft. above water, and consequently the passengers were required to embark before the lowering of the boats, thus endangering the operation and preventing the taking on of the maximum number the boats would hold.

"The boats at all times to be properly equipped with provisions, water, lamps, compasses, lights, etc. Life-saving boat-drills should be more frequent and thoroughly carried out, and officers should be armed at boat-drill.

"A greater reduction in speed in fog and ice, as the damage if a collision actually occurs is liable to be less.

"In conclusion, we suggest that an international conference should be called, and we recommend the passage of identical laws providing for the safety of all at sea. We urge the United States Government to take the initiative as soon as possible."

GRIM WIRELESS MESSAGE FROM SCENE OF DISASTER.

From the cable ship "Mackay-Bennett," which was hurried to the scene of the disaster to bring in any dead bodies that could be found, the following wireless message was received in New York on April 25 :—

Bodies are numerous in latitude 41.35 North, longitude 48.37 West, extending many miles both east and west. Mailships should give this region a wide berth.

The medical opinion is that death has been instantaneous in all the cases owing to the pressure when the bodies were drawn down in the vortex. We have been drifting in a dense fog since noon yesterday, and the total number of bodies picked up is 205.

We brought away all the embalming fluid in Halifax, which is enough for seventy. With a week's fine weather we think we should pretty well clear up the relics of the disaster.

In my opinion the majority of the bodies will never come to the surface.

NAVAL PATROL FOR LIFE SAVING.

A novel proposition has been put forward by Mr. E. S. May, of Chiswick, in a letter to the "Daily Chronicle" :—

"As there is always danger of collision with icebergs or between ships in fogs at sea," he writes, "may I make one or two suggestions for the prevention of loss of life ?

"First, that the Admiralty, instead of the Board of Trade, should be given power to deal with the saving of life at sea. It would be a glorious change in the history of a navy, which has for nearly a century of peace been engaged in huge preparations against an imaginary foe.

"Second, to select a few of our fastest cruisers (disarmed), fitted with every means for the rescue, reception, and comfort of those rescued. To patrol the routes of ocean-going vessels, etc., manned with crews of highly-trained tars, ready for any emergency, would obviate the necessity for carrying lifeboats or preservers. The 'wireless system' would speedily bring aid and relief, and this knowledge would of itself calm the fears of all in danger.

"Several nations might combine later on to have one international fleet, at

small cost to each, for the protection and saving of life, and for the sole protection of the world's commerce, as also for the police maintenance of the peace of the world. But England should have the honour of initiating this glorious work, and be the first in the field."

THE KAISER AND THE "TITANIC" WARNING.

The following semi-official statement has been issued at Berlin, says Reuter :—

"The Emperor has not confined the expression of his personal interest in the 'Titanic' catastrophe to warm telegrams of sympathy. He has taken up the questions arising from the great disaster with keen interest, and is in active telegraphic communication with authoritative personages concerned.

"His Imperial Majesty has ordered that a searching investigation, with a view to an extension of the life-saving precautions on board passenger ships, shall be begun forthwith in order to arrive at a basis for eventual international regulations on the subject. The results of the inquiry will be reported to him in personal audience by the Secretary of State for the Interior and the president of the Maritime Association.

SURVIVOR WHO WAS SUCKED DOWN WITH THE SHIP.

Colonel Gracie, of the United States Army, who jumped from the topmost deck of the "Titanic" when she sank, and was sucked down with her, has perhaps the most extraordinary story to tell.

Colonel Gracie, on reaching the surface, swam until he found a cork raft, and then helped to rescue others. He gives the exact time of the sinking of the "Titanic" as 2.22 a.m., which was the hour at which his watch was stopped by his leap into the sea.

"After sinking with the ship," he said, "it appeared to me as if I was propelled by some great force through the water. This might have been occasioned by explosions under the water, and I remembered fearful stories of people being boiled to death. The second officer has told me that he has had a similar experience.

"Innumerable thoughts of a personal nature having relation to mental telepathy flashed through my brain. I thought of those at home, as if my spirit might go to them to say 'Good-bye' for ever. Again and again I prayed for deliverance, although I felt sure that the end had come. I had the greatest difficulty in holding my breath until I came to the surface. I knew that once I inhaled the water would suffocate me. When I got under water I struck out with all my strength for the surface. I got to the air again after a time which seemed to me to be unending. There was nothing in sight save the ocean, dotted with and strewn with large masses of wreckage. Dying men and women all about me were groaning and crying piteously.

"The second officer and Mr. J. B. Thayer, jun., who were swimming near me, told me that just before my head appeared above the water one of the 'Titanic's' funnels separated and fell apart near me, scattering the bodies in the water. I saw wreckage everywhere, and all that came within reach I clung to."

Colonel Gracie relates how at last by moving from one piece of wreckage to another he reached the raft.

"Soon," he continued, "the raft became so full that it seemed as if she would sink if more came on board her. The crew, for self-preservation, had, therefore, to refuse to permit any others to climb on board. This was the most pathetic and horrible scene of all. The piteous cries of those around us ring in my ears, and I will remember them to my dying day.

"'Hold on to what you have, old boy,' we shouted to each man who tried to get on board. 'One more of you would sink us all.' Many of those whom we refused answered as they went to their death, 'Good luck! God bless you!' All the time we were buoyed up and sustained by the hope of rescue. We saw lights in all directions. Particularly frequent were some green lights, which, as we learned later, were rockets fired in the air by one of the 'Titanic's' boats. So we passed the night with the waves washing over and burying the raft deep in water.

"We prayed through all the weary night, and there never was a moment when our prayers did not rise above the waves. Men who seemed long ago to have forgotten how to address their Creator, recalled the prayers of their childhood, and murmured them over and over again. Together we said the Lord's Prayer again and again."

Lloyd's of London Press Ltd.
Sheepen Place, Colchester
Essex CO3 3LP, England

USA AND CANADA
Lloyd's of London Press Inc.
87 Terminal Drive, Plainview
New York, NY 10003 USA

GERMANY
Lloyd's of London Press
PO Box 11 23 47, Deichstrasse 41
2000 Hamburg 11, West Germany

SOUTH EAST ASIA
Lloyd's of London Press (Far East) Ltd.
1502 Chung Nam Building
1 Lockhart Road, Wanchai
Hong Kong

First published 1912 by Lloyd's Weekly News
This edition © 1985 Lloyd's of London Press Ltd.

British Library Cataloguing in Publication Data
The Deathless story of the Titanic : complete narrative.
1. Titanic (Ship)
363.1′23′091631   G530.T6

ISBN 1-85044-067-0

Printed in Great Britain by Lavenham Press Ltd.
Water Street, Lavenham, Suffolk

00395

The Remarkable
Body-Building Power
of BOVRIL

BOVRIL TAKEN

The
**Body-Building
Power**
of
BOVRIL
Taken.

In the recent experiments upon human subjects reported to the British Medical Association, an amount of Bovril proportionate to the small dark circle was proved to produce an increase in flesh and muscle corresponding to the large blue circle, showing the body-building power of Bovril to be from

10 to 20 times amount taken.